YOUR recipe could appear in our next cookbook!

Share your tried & true family favorites with us instantly at

www.gooseberrypatch.com

If you'd rather jot 'em down by hand, just mail this form to...

Gooseberry Patch • Cookbooks – Call for Recipes
PO Box 812 • Columbus, OH 43216-0812

If your recipe is selected for a book, you'll receive a FREE copy!

Please share only your original recipes or those that you have made your own over the years.

Recipe Name:

Number of Servings:

Any fond memories about this recipe? Special touches you like to add or handy shortcuts?

Ingredients (include specific measurements):

Instructions (continue on back if needed):

Special Code: **cookbookspage**

Over

Extra space for recipe if needed:

Tell us about yourself...

Your complete contact information is needed so that we can send you your FREE cookbook, if your recipe is published. Phone numbers and email addresses are kept private and will only be used if we have questions about your recipe.

Name:

Address:

City: State: Zip:

Email:

Daytime Phone:

Thank you! Vickie & Jo Ann

Spring & Summer
Recipes for Sharing

The freshest recipes from the country,
and easy-breezy ways to enjoy the simple
pleasures of spring & summer.

Gooseberry Patch

An imprint of Globe Pequot
64 South Main Street
Essex, CT 06426

www.gooseberrypatch.com
1·800·854·6673

Copyright 2023, Gooseberry Patch   978-1-62093-540-8

Do you have a tried & true recipe...

tip, craft or memory that you'd like to see featured in a **Gooseberry Patch** cookbook? Visit our website at **www.gooseberrypatch.com** and follow the easy steps to submit your favorite family recipe. Or send them to us at:

Gooseberry Patch
PO Box 812
Columbus, OH 43216-0812

Don't forget to include the number of servings your recipe makes, plus your name, address, phone number and email address. If we select your recipe, your name will appear right along with it... and you'll receive a **FREE** copy of the book!

Contents

Dedication

To everyone who loves the first spring flowers, shopping at the farmers' market, spending lazy days in the hammock and picnicking with family & friends.

Appreciation

A hearty thanks to each of you for sharing your tastiest sunny-weather recipes.

Brunch
in the Garden

Spring & Summer
Recipes for Sharing

Farm-Fresh Summer Frittata   *Amy Thomason Hunt*
Traphill, NC

I serve this tasty frittata for brunch or a light dinner. Nothing says summertime like garden-fresh vegetables to use in recipes!

6 to 8 slices bacon, cut into
    1/2-inch pieces
1/2 c. Tommy Toes or cherry
    tomatoes, halved
1/2 c. green pepper, diced
1/4 c. onion, diced

6 eggs, beaten
1/2 c. sour cream
salt and pepper to taste
1 c. finely shredded Cheddar
    or Colby cheese

Cook bacon in a cast-iron skillet over medium heat for 4 minutes. Drain bacon on paper towels; partially drain drippings in skillet. Return bacon to skillet; add tomatoes, green pepper and onion. Cook for 3 minutes, or until pepper and onion are crisp-tender. Remove from heat. In a medium bowl, whisk together eggs, sour cream and seasonings until well blended. Add to vegetables in skillet and mix well. (At this point, if skillet isn't oven-proof, transfer mixture to a 9" round baking pan.) Top with cheese; cover with aluminum foil. Bake at 350 degrees for 18 to 25 minutes, until a knife inserted in the center comes out clean. Cut into wedges. Serves 6.

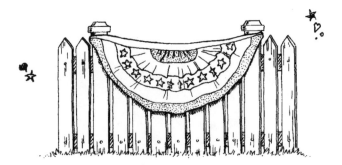

Make the most of a warm spring morning...take breakfast outdoors! Toss a quilt over the table and serve some warm muffins with homemade jam and fresh fruit.

Brunch
in the Garden

Lisa's Peach Pie Muffins
Lisa Ann Panzino DiNunzio
Vineland, NJ

Peach pie meets muffins...yes, please!

1-3/4 c. all-purpose flour
3/4 c. turbinado sugar or light
   brown sugar, packed
2 T. baking powder
2 t. cinnamon
1/2 t. sea salt
3/4 c. milk

1/3 c. oil
1 egg, beaten
1 t. vanilla extract
1 c. ripe peaches, peeled, pitted
   and diced
Optional: additional sugar

In a large bowl, combine flour, sugar, baking powder, cinnamon and salt. Stir until combined; set aside. In a separate bowl, mix together milk, oil, egg and vanilla. Stir milk mixture into flour mixture, just until combined. Gently stir in peaches. Fill greased or paper-lined muffin cups with batter, 3/4 full. Sprinkle muffin tops with additional sugar, if desired. Bake at 400 degrees for 20 minutes, or until a toothpick inserted into the center comes out clean. Makes one dozen.

Wake everyone up to colorful pottery on the breakfast table... so cheery. Search tag sales for whimsical hens on nests or cream pitcher cows. What treasures!

Spring & Summer
Recipes for Sharing

Strawberry-Rhubarb Coffee Cake

Christy Easter
Dover, NH

There is a rhubarb patch in my father's garden that grows every year, and has since I was a little girl. Every spring, this is the first recipe I make with the new crop. It is delicious served warm or at room temperature...there are usually no leftovers!

3-1/2 c. all-purpose flour, divided	1-1/4 c. butter, divided
1 t. baking powder	1-1/2 c. sugar, divided
1 t. baking soda	2 eggs
1 t. salt	1 c. buttermilk
	1 t. vanilla extract

Prepare Fruit Filling; set aside. In a large bowl, sift together 3 cups flour, baking powder, baking soda and salt; set aside. In the bowl of a stand mixer, beat together one cup butter and one cup sugar until fluffy. Add eggs, one at a time, beating well after each addition. Turn mixer to low speed. Add flour mixture to butter mixture in 3 batches, alternating with buttermilk. Add vanilla; beat just until batter is combined. Batter will be very thick; do not overbeat. Spread half of batter in a lightly greased 13"x9" baking pan. Spoon Fruit Filling over batter in pan. Using a large spoon, add remaining batter in dollops over fruit. For crumb topping, combine remaining flour, butter and sugar in a food processor; process until coarse crumbs form. Sprinkle evenly over fruit. Bake at 350 degrees for 40 to 50 minutes. Makes 12 servings.

Fruit Filling:

3 c. rhubarb, cut into one-inch pieces	1 c. sugar
	2 T. lemon juice
1 lb. fresh strawberries, hulled and sliced	1/2 c. cornstarch
	small amount water

Combine fruits and sugar in a saucepan over medium heat. In a small bowl, mix lemon juice and cornstarch into a paste, adding a little water until mixture is smooth. Add to fruit mixture. Cook and stir for about 5 minutes, until mixture thickens, watching closely.

Brunch
in the Garden

Crabmeat Quiche

Linda Belon
Wintersville, OH

A delicious breakfast treat! Serve with fruit salad.

2 eggs, beaten
1/2 c. mayonnaise
2 T. all-purpose flour
1/2 c. milk
1 c. fresh or canned crabmeat,
    drained and flaked

1 c. Swiss cheese, diced
1/2 c. green onions, chopped
9-inch pie crust, unbaked

In a large bowl, beat together eggs, mayonnaise, flour and milk until well blended. Stir in crabmeat, cheese and onion. Spread into pie crust. Bake at 350 degrees for 40 to 45 minutes, until a knife tip inserted in the center comes out clean. Cut into wedges. Makes 6 to 8 servings.

Orange Julius

Doreen Knapp
Stanfordville, NY

This recipe is my Auntie Irene's. I had asked for her cookbook after she passed. It's filled with handwritten treasures. I'm thankful that I have it and I love to see her handwriting again.

6-oz. can frozen orange
    juice concentrate
1 c. milk
1 c. water

1/4 c. sugar
1 t. vanilla extract
6 to 8 ice cubes

Combine all ingredients in a blender. Process until well blended; divide among 3 tall glasses. Makes 3 servings.

Sweet April showers
Do bring May flowers.

–Thomas Tusser

Spring & Summer
Recipes for Sharing

Grilled French Toast

Mary Kelly
Jefferson City, MO

Every summer, our family grills for at least the four nights leading up to and including the 4th of July. It's been fondly dubbed "Grillfest." One morning, my husband, daughter and I get up early, fire up the charcoal grill and make this yummy breakfast. The smoky taste of this French toast makes it unique, especially when topped with fresh berries, chopped pecans, a dollop of whipped cream, a drizzle of maple syrup and of course, a tiny American flag. While the fire is still hot, we also grill dinner for that evening.

5 eggs, beaten
1/4 c. light brown sugar, packed
1/4 t. cinnamon
2 t. vanilla extract
1-1/2 c. milk

10 slices French bread,
   3/4-inch thick
Garnish: fresh strawberries and
   blueberries, chopped pecans,
   whipped cream, maple syrup

In a wide, shallow bowl, whisk together eggs, brown sugar, cinnamon and vanilla. Whisk in milk. Coat both sides of bread slices with egg mixture. Lightly oil grill grate. Add bread slices to the grill and cover. Grill over medium heat until lightly golden, about 2 to 3 minutes per side. Garnish as desired. Serves 5.

For a fruity cream cheese spread, combine an 8-ounce package of softened cream cheese with 1/4 cup of your favorite fruit preserves. Stir until smooth. So delicious on bagels and muffins!

Brunch
in the Garden

Kathy's Egg Puff

Kathy Grashoff
Fort Wayne, IN

*Easter's coming! Actually, this dish is great for any gathering.
It's especially nice when you have guests.*

1/4 c. butter
1 doz. eggs, beaten
1/2 c. all-purpose flour
1 t. baking powder

2 c. cottage cheese
16-oz. pkg. shredded Monterey
   Jack cheese

Place butter in a 13"x9" baking pan; place in 350-degree oven until melted. Meanwhile, in a blender, blend eggs, flour and baking powder for one minute, or until smooth. Transfer mixture to a bowl; fold in cheeses. Remove pan from oven; pour egg mixture over melted butter. Bake, uncovered, at 350 degrees for 30 minutes, or until center is set. Let stand 10 minutes; cut into squares. Makes 12 servings.

Babchi's Glazed Bacon

Paula Marchesi
Auburn, PA

*I love to serve this bacon at family gatherings. It's great chopped
and sprinkled over waffles and pancakes, or over salads and
burgers. I always double the recipe and freeze half for later.*

1 lb. sliced bacon
1 c. brown sugar, packed
1/4 c. white wine or
   unsweetened apple juice

2 T. horseradish mustard
Optional: pepper to taste

Arrange bacon slices on a wire rack; set in an ungreased 15"x10" jelly-roll pan. Bake at 350 degrees for 10 minutes; drain and set aside. In a bowl, combine brown sugar, wine or apple juice and mustard; drizzle half of mixture over bacon. Season with pepper, if desired. Return to oven for 10 minutes. Turn slices over and drizzle with remaining mustard; bake for another 10 minutes. Transfer slices to wax paper; serve warm. Serves 8.

Spring & Summer
Recipes for Sharing

Hawaiian Breakfast Hash

Courtney Stultz
Weir, KS

This tasty twist on breakfast hashbrowns is full of flavor!
It's also full of possibilities. Top with a poached egg or add
some fresh spinach for an extra twist.

4 slices bacon
1 T. coconut oil
2 to 3 sweet potatoes, peeled
   and diced
2 c. fresh or canned
   pineapple, diced

1/4 t. chili powder
1/4 t. paprika
1/4 t. cinnamon
1 t. sea salt
1/2 t. pepper

In a large skillet over medium heat, cook bacon until crisp. Remove bacon to a paper towel-lined plate. Drain skillet; add coconut oil and sweet potatoes. Sauté for about 15 minutes, stirring frequently. Add pineapple and seasonings; crumble bacon and add to skillet. Sauté for another 5 to 8 minutes, until potatoes are tender and golden. Makes 4 servings.

Tuck cut flowers into a vintage teapot for a delightful table decoration. Try old-fashioned blooms like daisies, coreopsis, bachelor buttons, zinnia and larkspur.

Brunch
in the Garden

Banana-Nut Muffins with Coconut

Jahaira Cormier
Westampton, NJ

*A tropical delight! The riper the banana,
the better it is for this recipe.*

5 very ripe bananas
3/4 c. sugar
1/2 c. brown sugar, packed
1 egg, beaten
1/2 c. butter, melted
1-1/2 c. all-purpose flour

1 t. baking powder
1 t. baking soda
1/2 c. shredded sweetened
   coconut
1/2 c. chopped walnuts

Mash bananas in a large bowl. Add sugars, egg and melted butter; mix well and set aside. In a separate bowl, mix flour, baking powder and baking soda. With an electric mixer on medium speed, or by hand, gradually add flour mixture to banana mixture. Fold in coconut and walnuts. Pour batter into 18 paper-lined or well-greased muffin cups, filling 3/4 full. Bake at 350 degrees for 25 to 30 minutes. Makes 1-1/2 dozen.

Treat yourself to a melon bowl for breakfast. Cut a ripe cantaloupe or honeydew in half, scoop out the seeds and fill with yogurt, granola, berries and a drizzle of honey.

Spring & Summer
Recipes for Sharing

Cheesy Baked Eggs

Linda Murray
Brentwood, NH

I have been making this for Christmas morning breakfast for over 30 years, and occasionally for Easter breakfast. Now my daughter and granddaughter make this dish too. This recipe allows for one egg per person, but I've found that women usually eat two eggs and men can usually devour as many as four eggs...so plan accordingly!

2 10-3/4 oz. cans cream of
    chicken soup
1/2 c. milk
4 t. onion, grated
1 t. mustard
2-1/2 c. shredded sharp
    Cheddar cheese

1 doz. whole eggs
12 slices French bread,
    1/2-inch thick
softened butter to taste

In a saucepan, combine chicken soup, milk, onion and mustard. Cook and stir over medium heat until well blended and heated through. Remove from heat; add cheese and stir until melted. Spread half of mixture in a lightly greased 13"x9" baking pan; break eggs over sauce. Spoon remaining sauce around eggs. Spread bread slices on both sides with butter; cut slices in half diagonally. Stand half-slices of bread around edges of pan. Bake, uncovered, at 350 degrees for about 30 minutes, until eggs are set. Makes 12 servings.

Favorite breakfast foods are perfect for a light supper in summertime. A simple omelet or frittata is perfect. Just add a basket of muffins, fresh fruit and a pitcher of ice tea.

Brunch
in the Garden

Blueberry Coffee Cake

Karen Wald
Dalton, OH

This is a tried & true family recipe that I have enjoyed making for many years. It is quick& easy to put together and tastes extra spectacular warm from the oven.

1/4 c. canola oil	1/2 c. whole-wheat flour
1 egg, beaten	2 t. baking powder
3/4 c. sugar	1/2 t. salt
1/2 c. buttermilk	2 c. frozen blueberries
1-1/2 c. all-purpose flour	

Combine Topping ingredients and set aside. In a bowl, whisk together canola oil, egg and sugar; stir in buttermilk and set aside. In another bowl, combine flours, baking powder and salt. Mix lightly and add to oil mixture; stir just until blended. Gently stir in frozen blueberries. Spread batter in a greased 9"x9" baking pan. Sprinkle with topping. Bake at 375 degrees for about 25 minutes. Cut into squares. Makes 9 servings.

Topping:

1/4 c. butter, softened	1/3 c. all-purpose flour
1/2 c. sugar	1/2 t. cinnamon

Blend together all ingredients.

Surprise Mom with breakfast in bed...and it doesn't have to be just on Mothers' Day! Fill a tray with breakfast goodies, the morning paper and a bright blossom tucked into an egg cup.

Spring & Summer
Recipes for Sharing

Spinach & Mushroom
Breakfast Bake

JoAnn
Gooseberry Patch

Great for brunch in spring and summer! A time-saver, too...
just put it all together the night before, then pop it in the oven
in the morning. Just add some pastries and serve.

1/4 c. butter, melted
6 slices bread, crusts removed
1 c. shredded mozzarella cheese
1 c. shredded Cheddar cheese
5 eggs, beaten
2 c. half-and-half
1 t. salt

1/2 t. pepper
1 to 2 T. butter, sliced
1 c. onion, chopped
1/2 lb. sliced mushrooms
10-oz. pkg. frozen spinach,
thawed and drained

Spread melted butter in a 13"x9" baking pan. Tear bread into pieces;
sprinkle over butter. Combine cheeses in a bowl; sprinkle 1-1/2 cups
cheese mixture over bread and set aside. In a bowl, whisk together
eggs, half-and-half and seasonings. Pour over cheese. Cover and chill
8 hours or overnight. At the same time, melt sliced butter in a skillet
over medium heat, sauté onion and mushrooms until tender. Remove
to a bowl; cover and refrigerate overnight. In the morning, uncover pan
with bread. Spread chilled mushroom mixture and spinach over top;
sprinkle with remaining cheese. Bake, uncovered, at 350 degrees for
45 to 50 minutes, until golden and set in the center. Serves 6 to 8.

Broiled tomatoes are a tasty, quick garnish for egg dishes. Arrange
tomato halves on a broiler pan. Drizzle lightly with olive oil;
season with salt and pepper. Broil until tender, 2 to 3 minutes.

Brunch
in the Garden

French Vanilla Cinnamon Roll Cake

Nina Jones
Springfield, OH

This is an Easter morning favorite...it's a lot easier than homemade cinnamon rolls! Everyone loves the yummy, ooey-gooey icing.

15-1/4 oz. pkg. French vanilla
   cake mix
4 eggs, beaten

3/4 c. oil
1 c. sour cream

Combine all ingredients in a large bowl. Beat with an electric mixer on medium speed for 2 minutes, or well combined. Pour batter into a greased 13"x9" baking pan. Spooon Cinnamon Topping over batter. With a knife, swirl topping mixture into batter. Bake at 350 degrees for 30 to 40 minutes. Spoon Icing over warm cake; spread with a spatula to cover top of cake. Cut into squares. Serves 12.

Cinnamon Topping:

1 c. butter, melted
1 c. brown sugar, packed
1 T. cinnamon

1/4 t. nutmeg
1 t. vanilla extract

Combine all ingredients; stir until well combined.

Icing:

2 c. powdered sugar
1/4 c. milk

1 t. vanilla extract

Mix ingredients until well combined and smooth.

Honey comes in lots of flavor varieties. Seek out a local beekeeper at the farmers' market and try a few samples. You may find a new favorite!

Spring & Summer
Recipes for Sharing

Blueberry-White Chocolate Chip Scones

Eleanor Dionne
Beverly, MA

This tried & true recipe is perfect for a Mothers' Day brunch or an afternoon tea on a sunny day.

2 c. all-purpose flour
1/3 c. plus 2 T. sugar, divided
1 t. baking powder
1/2 t. baking soda
1/2 teaspoon salt
5 T. chilled butter, diced

3/4 c. white chocolate chips
3/4 c. fresh blueberries
3/4 c. buttermilk
1 egg yolk
1 t. vanilla extract

In a large bowl, mix flour, 1/3 cup sugar, baking powder, baking soda and salt. Add diced butter. Mix with a pastry blender until butter is reduced to the size of grains of rice. Mix in chocolate chips and blueberries; set aside. In another bowl, whisk together buttermilk, egg yolk and vanilla. Add buttermilk mixture to flour mixture; stir until dough forms a ball. Place dough on a lightly floured surface and press into an 8-inch circle. Cut into 8 wedges; sprinkle with remaining sugar. Transfer wedges to to a parchment paper-lined baking sheet. Bake at 375 degrees for 15 to 20 minutes. Serve warm. Makes 8 scones.

For Mothers' Day, a basket of homemade scones makes a delightful gift. Tuck in jars of creamy spread and strawberry jam to complete the surprise.

Brunch
in the Garden

Easy Fresh Fruit Salad

Kathy Courington
Canton, GA

I love this salad because I can do most of it the night before, and then toss it together the next morning. Always a favorite!

8 to 10 c. assorted fresh
   melon cubes
1 to 2 T. light corn syrup
2 c. fresh pineapple cubes

1 pt. fresh strawberries, hulled
   and sliced
2 oranges, peeled and sectioned
Optional: fresh mint leaves

In a large bowl, combine melon cubes and corn syrup; toss to coat. Cover and refrigerate overnight. Just before serving, add remaining fruit; stir gently. Garnish with mint, if desired. Serves 8 to 10.

Old English Devonshire Cream Dip

Lynda Hart
Bluffdale, UT

This dip is rich and delicious. It's wonderful with strawberries, pineapple chunks, apple slices, orange segments, grapes and sliced bananas. It's also tasty on biscuits and scones, topped with jam.

8-oz. pkg. cream cheese,
   softened
3/4 c. whipping cream

1/2 t. vanilla extract
1 t. sugar

In a bowl, beat cream cheese with an electric mixer on high speed until fluffy. Beat in cream, a little at a time, to desired consistency. Stir in vanilla and sugar. Cover and chill before serving. Makes about 1-1/2 cups.

Set the breakfast table the night before...enjoy a relaxed breakfast in the morning!

Spring & Summer
Recipes for Sharing

Biscuits & Gravy Casserole
Vicki Van Donselaar
Cedar, IA

*This is a great dish to take to an Easter sunrise service at church,
or to serve at a family brunch.*

1 lb. ground pork sausage
2 2-3/4 oz. pkgs. peppered
  gravy mix
12-oz. tube refrigerated
  buttermilk biscuits, cut into
  one-inch pieces

1 c. shredded Cheddar cheese
6 eggs, beaten
1/2 c. milk
salt and pepper to taste

Brown sausage in a skillet over medium heat; drain. Meanwhile,
prepare gravy according to package directions. To assemble, scatter
biscuit pieces evenly in a buttered 13"x9" baking pan. Scatter sausage
evenly over biscuit pieces; top with cheese. Whisk together eggs, milk,
salt and pepper; pour evenly into pan. Spoon warm gravy evenly over
eggs. Bake, uncovered, at 350 degrees for 30 to 40 minutes, until eggs
are set. Cut into squares and serve. Serves 15.

The summer of 2019, we spent our family vacation traveling over
20 hours (each way!) in the car, driving from West Virginia to
Minnesota to visit our Uncle Earl and Aunt Jennifer. Along the way,
we ate at many delicious restaurants, but none compared to Aunt
Jennifer's breakfast spreads. Each morning we woke to the smell of
fresh-brewed coffee and the sound of genuine joy. Their dining
room table was covered in a checked tablecloth and set with the
most beautiful vintage china dishes. Although the main course
changed daily, you knew there would always be glasses of cold
orange juice, overflowing bowls of berries and great conversation!
–Monica Britt, Fairdale, WV

Brunch
in the Garden

Campers' Breakfast Hash

Carolyn Deckard
Bedford, IN

*Whenever we go camping with family and friends, I'm asked
to make this hearty breakfast. It really sets us up for
a day of hiking and enjoying the great outdoors.*

1/4 c. butter, cubed
2 20-oz. pkgs. refrigerated
   shredded hashbrown
   potatoes
6.4-oz. pkg. brown & serve
   sausage links, sliced
   1/2-inch thick

1/4 c. onion, chopped
1/4 c. green pepper, chopped
1 doz. eggs, lightly beaten
salt and pepper to taste
1 c. shredded Cheddar cheese

Melt butter in a large skillet over medium heat. Add potatoes, sausages, onion and green pepper. Cook, uncovered, over medium heat for 10 to 15 minutes, or until potatoes are lightly golden, turning once. Push potato mixture to the sides of pan; pour eggs into the center. Cook and stir over medium heat until eggs are completely set. Season with salt and pepper. Reduce heat to medium-low; stir eggs into potato mixture. Top with cheese. Cover and cook for one to 2 minutes, until cheese is melted. Serves 8.

Stir up a refreshing fruit beverage for breakfast. Combine
equal parts chilled orange juice, pomegranate juice and
club soda. Serve over ice.

Spring & Summer
Recipes for Sharing

Strawberry-Filled French Toast

Wendy Ball
Battle Creek, MI

A long time ago, our family visited Disney World and ate a wonderful stuffed French toast there. Over the years, as the kids grew up, we would make stuffed French toast. It was always the best when fruit was in season. To us, this tastes like summer and brings back those memories of our vacation together.

1 large loaf egg bread or
   challah bread
6 eggs, beaten
1/2 c. milk

1/2 t. salt
1 T. butter
Garnish: powdered sugar

Make Strawberry Filling; spoon into a one-gallon plastic zipping bag and set aside. Cut loaf into 6, 2-inch slices; save ends for another recipe. Cut a pocket into side of each slice; do not cut all the way through. Cut at least one inch off one tip of filling bag. Squeeze 1/4 cup filling into each bread slice; flatten slightly to seal pocket. In a shallow bowl, whisk together eggs, milk and salt until foamy; set aside. Melt butter in a large skillet over medium heat. For each serving, dip one slice of filled bread into egg mixture; turn once to coat and place in skillet. Cook for about 3 to 4 minutes; turn and cook the other side for 3 to 4 minutes longer, until golden. Transfer to a wire rack set on a baking sheet; set in 200-degree oven until ready to serve. Dust with powdered sugar and serve. Serves 6.

Strawberry Filling:

2 8-oz. pkgs. cream cheese,
   softened
1/2 c. sugar
1 T. vanilla extract

1/2 t. cinnamon
16-oz. pkg. frozen no-sugar-
   added strawberries, thawed
   and drained

Beat cream cheese and sugar until fluffy; add vanilla and cinnamon. Chop strawberries; fold into mixture.

Brunch
in the Garden

Cream Cheese Sausage Balls

Jennifer Dorward
Winder, GA

We love these at breakfast on special days, served alongside some cheesy scrambled eggs. They make a fantastic appetizer too, and can even be served room temperature at a picnic! They are always a huge hit in our home. Sometimes I even make a double batch! The balls can be frozen, unbaked, and popped in the oven later. Just add a few more minutes to the baking time.

1 lb. regular or hot ground
   pork sausage
8-oz. pkg. cream cheese,
   softened

1-1/4 c. biscuit baking mix
1 c. shredded Cheddar cheese
Optional: hot pepper sauce

Combine all ingredients except hot sauce in a large bowl. Mix until well combined. This mixture is sticky and works best with an electric mixer with a dough hook attachment. Roll into one-inch balls, using a small melon baller or cookie scoop. Arrange balls on an ungreased rimmed baking sheet. Bake at 400 degrees for 20 minutes. Serve with hot sauce for dipping, if desired. Makes about 3-1/2 dozen.

Hosting a family reunion? Bring out all the family photo albums.
Sure to spark conversation as your guests look at pictures
they haven't seen in years!

Spring & Summer
Recipes for Sharing

Breakfast Dump Pie

Peg Scott
Turtle Creek, PA

There were times when we needed to be frugal and this recipe always came in handy. Sometimes I put tomatoes on top. You can add mushrooms also. Play with this recipe and have fun!

2 russet potatoes, diced
2 t. water
1 c. cooked ham, sausage or
  bacon, chopped
1/2 c. onion, diced

1 c. favorite shredded cheese
4 eggs, beaten
1 c. milk
salt and pepper to taste

Combine potatoes and water in a microwave-safe bowl; microwave just until softened. Spread potatoes in a greased 9" pie plate. Top with meat, onion and cheese; set aside. In another bowl, beat together eggs and milk. Pour egg mixture over potato mixture; season with salt and pepper. Bake, uncovered, at 350 degrees for 45 minutes. Let cool for 10 minutes; cut into wedges. Serves 6.

Foolproof Hollandaise Sauce

Doreen Knapp
Stanfordville, NY

Great for dressing up poached eggs for Easter brunch and other special occasions...foolproof and delicious!

2 egg yolks, room temperature
1/4 c. whipping cream
1/4 c. butter, softened

juice of 1 lemon
salt and pepper to taste

In the top of a double boiler, stir together egg yolks, cream and butter. Cook over medium-low heat for about 15 minutes, stirring constantly, until consistency changes and thickens. Just before serving, stir in lemon juice; season with salt and pepper. Serve warm. Makes 4 servings.

Fill a large basket with bright oranges for
a beautiful breakfast centerpiece.

Brunch
in the Garden

Overnight Sticky Buns

Rebecca Meadows
Hinton, WV

This recipe is perfect for breakfast...prepare and clean up the night before. It's great when you have company and don't want to cook the morning away. Instead you can socialize with your guests, drink your coffee or tea and enjoy eating a yummy sticky bun. I've also made this for those early mornings my husband is leaving on a fishing trip. While he packs his gear in the truck, I can pop these in the oven and soon they're ready to go.

18 to 20 frozen yeast dinner rolls
3.4-oz. pkg. cook & serve
   butterscotch pudding mix

1/2 c. brown sugar, packed
1 t. cinnamon
1/2 c. butter, melted

Layer frozen rolls in a greased Bundt® pan; set aside. In a bowl, combine dry pudding mix, brown sugar and cinnamon. Mix well; sprinkle over frozen rolls. Drizzle with melted butter. Cover pan with plastic wrap; let rolls rise overnight at room temperature. The next morning, remove plastic wrap. Bake at 350 degrees for 20 to 25 minutes, until golden. Turn buns out onto a plate and serve. Makes 18 to 20 buns.

Deliver a tray of your favorite breakfast goodies to
the teachers' lounge on the last day of school...
it's sure to be appreciated!

Spring & Summer
Recipes for Sharing

Sweet Corn Frittata with Bacon & Swiss

Dale Duncan
Waterloo, IA

Here in Iowa, we like our sweet corn any way it's served! This is a delicious light dish for summer brunch or lunch. If you're using fresh corn on the cob, you'll need two ears. Add a spoonful of diced jalapeño pepper, if you like a little heat.

8 eggs, beaten
1/4 c. whole milk
1-1/4 c. shredded Swiss
   cheese, divided
salt and pepper to taste

1 t. olive oil
4 thick-cut slices bacon, diced
1-1/2 c. corn, thawed if frozen
5 green onions, coarsely chopped

In a large bowl, whisk together eggs and milk; stir in half of cheese. Season with salt and pepper; set aside. Heat oil in a cast-iron skillet over medium-high heat. Cook bacon for 4 minutes, or until lightly golden but not crisp. Transfer bacon to a paper towel–lined plate; reserve one tablespoon drippings in pan. Add corn and onions to skillet. Cook for 4 minutes or until tender, stirring occasionally. Add eggs and cook for 4 minutes, stirring occasionally, just until eggs are lightly set. Top with bacon and remaining cheese. Place skillet on oven rack, 4 inches below broiler. Broil for several minutes, watching closely, until set on top and lightly golden. Cut into wedges and serve immediately. Makes 4 servings.

Invite your best friend over for a morning brunch. It's a great way to get caught up on each other's summer plans while sharing tasty breakfast foods and a pot of hot tea!

Brunch
in the Garden

Spinach Scramble

Susan Kieboam
Ontario, Canada

My family enjoys spinach quiche, but most mornings are too busy to bake a quiche from scratch. So I incorporated the flavors into a quick-to-fix deconstructed version of a spinach quiche. It's become a family favorite. This recipe serves one, but is easy to adjust for more.

1/4 c. milk	2 eggs, beaten
1 T. plus 1/8 t. all-purpose flour	1/4 c. shredded Cheddar cheese
1 slice bacon, diced	1 T. grated Parmesan cheese
3/4 c. fresh spinach, torn	salt to taste

Add milk to a small bowl; whisk in flour until smooth. Set aside. Cook bacon in a small skillet over medium heat; do not drain. Add spinach; cook and stir until wilted, one to 2 minutes. Add eggs to skillet; cook and stir until still slightly runny. Add milk mixture to egg mixture; cook and stir to desired creamy consistency. (You may not need all of milk mixture.) Fold in cheeses just until melted, less than one minute. Season with salt; turn onto a plate. Serves one.

Loaded Avocado Toast

Chaplain Leslie Kirzner
Boonton, NJ

One day, I was inspired to use whatever ingredients I found in my kitchen to create "à la mode" avocado toast. My husband loved it!

1 c. cherry tomatoes, halved	4 slices bread, toasted
olive oil and honey to taste	everything bagel seasoning
salt and pepper to taste	to taste
6 T. guacamole	8 t. balsamic glaze
2 T. fresh basil, torn	

Spread tomato halves on an ungreased baking sheet. Bake at 375 degrees for 30 minutes. Drizzle tomatoes with olive oil and honey; season with salt and pepper. Divide guacamole, tomatoes and basil evenly among toast slices. Sprinkle with seasoning; drizzle with balsamic glaze and serve. Serves 2.

Spring & Summer
Recipes for Sharing

Berry Good Streusel Muffins

Melinda Daniels
Lewiston, ID

This is a family favorite recipe that doesn't last a day around here! I love to make these around the 4th of July, when the berries are at their peak and the muffins seem to be showing their patriotism with the red, white and blue colors.

2-1/2 c. all-purpose flour
2-1/2 t. baking powder
1 c. strawberries, thawed
   if frozen
1 c. blueberries, thawed if frozen
2 eggs, beaten

1-1/4 c. sugar
1/4 c. butter, melted and
   cooled slightly
1/4 c. sour cream
1 c. buttermilk
2 t. lemon juice

In a large bowl, mix together flour and baking powder. Add berries; toss to coat and set aside. In another bowl, whisk together eggs and sugar until well combined. Slowly stir in melted butter and sour cream; stir in buttermilk and lemon juice. Using a spatula, mix flour mixture into egg mixture; do not overmix. Batter will be lumpy and may seem a little on the wet side. Spoon batter into greased or paper-lined muffin cups, filling 3/4 full. Sprinkle with Streusel Topping. Bake at 425 degrees for 15 to 17 minutes, until golden and a toothpick inserted in the center tests clean. Makes 2 dozen.

Streusel Topping:

3 T. sugar
3 T. brown sugar, packed
1/3 c. all-purpose flour

3 T. butter, melted, or more
   as needed

Combine sugars and flour; mix well. Slowly stir in melted butter until mixture forms pea-like shapes.

Brunch
in the Garden

Mini Spinach-Artichoke Frittatas

Bethany Scott
Huntsville, AZ

Perfect for a brunch spread! These little morsels can even be baked ahead of time, cooled and chilled up to 4 hours. To reheat for serving, cover loosely with foil and bake at 350 degrees for 5 to 10 minutes, just until warmed.

6 eggs, beaten
3/4 c. grated Parmesan cheese
1/4 c. mayonnaise
1 T. all-purpose flour
1 T. Dijon mustard
1/2 t. pepper

14-oz. can artichoke hearts,
   drained and chopped
10-oz. pkg. frozen chopped
   spinach, thawed and drained
3 green onions, thinly sliced
1/3 c. red pepper, finely chopped

In a large bowl, combine eggs, Parmesan cheese, mayonnaise, flour, mustard and pepper. Whisk until well blended. Add remaining ingredients; mix well. Spoon 1-1/2 tablespoons of mixture into each of 32 mini muffin cups coated with non-stick vegetable spray. Bake at 350 degrees for 15 to 18 minutes, until a toothpick inserted in center comes out clean. Makes about 2-1/2 dozen.

Breakfast on the go! Any egg dish turns into a portable breakfast when spooned into a pita half, or rolled up in a tortilla. Wrap it in a napkin and off you go!

Saucijsjes

Joyce Keeling
Springfield, MO

I grew up in the Dutch community of Pella, Iowa, where these Saucijsjes or "Pigs-in-a-Blanket" were served often for afternoon coffee times, wedding and baby showers, or as a quick grab & go breakfast. Thousands were made and sold every May at booths at the annual Tulip Festival. The dough is so flaky and delicious, as the sausage juices bake right into it. They were a favorite of mine as a child, and are now favorites of my own children and grandchildren.

2 c. all-purpose flour	1/2 c. shortening
2 t. baking powder	1 egg
1/2 t. salt	1/2 c. milk, or as needed

In a bowl, sift together flour, baking powder and salt. Cut in shortening until small crumbs form; set aside. Beat egg in a measuring cup. Add enough milk to equal 3/4 cup; add to flour mixture and blend well. Knead dough 8 to 10 times on a lightly floured board. Divide dough into 2 parts. Roll out each part to the thickness of a pie crust. Cut 15 circles of dough from each part with a 3-inch round biscuit cutter. Place a Pork Filling roll in the center of each pastry circle; fold edges together and seal, totally encasing the sausage. Arrange on ungreased baking sheets. Bake at 350 degrees for 40 minutes, to ensure pork is cooked thoroughly. Remove from oven; transfer to a platter. Serve hot or cold; may be frozen and reheated before serving. Makes 30 rolls.

Pork Filling:

1 lb. lean pork sausage	2 T. milk
1/2 lb. lean ground beef	salt & pepper to taste
1/4 c. dry bread crumbs	

Blend together all ingredients. Form into 30 small rolls, the size of small breakfast sausages.

Brunch
in the Garden

Baked French Toast Sandwiches
Janis Parr
Ontario, Canada

These French toast sandwiches make breakfast delicious and nutritious. Convenient too, since they're assembled the night before. Use whatever kind of fruit preserves you like.

1/2 c. butter, melted
1/2 c. brown sugar, packed
1/4 c. honey
1/4 to 1/2 c. butter, softened
12 thin slices sandwich bread
1 c. favorite fruit preserves

6 eggs, beaten
1/2 c. light cream or 3% milk
1/2 t. cinnamon
1/8 t. ground ginger
Optional: warmed maple syrup

In a small bowl, stir together melted butter, brown sugar and honey. Spoon into a buttered 13"x9" baking pan with 2" deep sides. Spread over bottom and sides of pan; set aside. Lightly spread one side of each bread slice with softened butter. Spread 6 slices with preserves; top with remaining slices. Arrange sandwiches close together in pan. In a small bowl, whisk together eggs, milk and spices; pour evenly over sandwiches. Cover and refrigerate overnight. Uncover and bake at 350 degrees for 30 minutes, or until golden. If desired, drizzle with warmed maple syrup. Cut apart and remove whole sandwiches; serve hot. Makes 4 to 6 sandwiches.

Are kids are eager to skip breakfast, get outside and start playing? Tempt them with grilled cheese sandwiches for breakfast, toasted on a waffle iron instead of a griddle. Grilled peanut butter sammies are tasty too.

Spring & Summer
Recipes for Sharing

Baked Walnut French Toast

Beckie Apple
Grannis, AR

A great twist on classic French toast! Good for breakfast...great for brunch. I like this because it's a smaller recipe for a smaller family.

4 c. French bread, cut into
   1-1/2 inch cubes
6 T. margarine, sliced and
   divided
1/2 c. brown sugar, packed
1/4 c. walnuts, finely diced
3 eggs, beaten

1-1/2 c. whole milk
1/2 c. sugar
1 T. vanilla extract
1 t. cinnamon
1/8 t. nutmeg
Garnish: pancake syrup

Spread bread cubes evenly on an ungreased baking sheet. Bake at 350 degrees for 5 to 10 minutes, just until lightly toasted; set aside. Meanwhile, coat an 8"x8" pan with non-stick vegetable spray. Add 4 tablespoons margarine to pan; set in oven just until melted. Spread bread cubes evenly over margarine in pan; sprinkle brown sugar and walnuts over bread. Dice remaining margarine and scatter over bread; set aside. In a bowl, whisk together eggs, milk, sugar, vanilla and spices until well mixed and frothy. Pour evenly over bread. Bake, uncovered, at 350 degrees for 35 minutes, or until golden. Serve warm, topped with syrup. Serves 4 to 6.

Take the kids to a nearby pick-your-own peach orchard or strawberry farm. Give them each a bucket and pretend not to notice when they nibble on their pickings!

Brunch
in the Garden

30-Minute Orange Knots

*Ann Farris
Biscoe, AR*

*These are so yummy and good! I love to bake...
this is baking made easy.*

16-oz. tube refrigerated biscuits,
   cut in half
3 T. butter, melted
2 T. sugar

1 T. plus 1 t. orange zest, divided
1/2 c. powdered sugar
1 T orange juice

Roll each half-biscuit into a rope. Tie each rope in a loose knot, tucking ends underneath the knot. Arrange knots on parchment-paper lined baking sheets; brush with melted butter. In a shallow bowl, combine sugar and one tablespoon orange zest. Dip buttered tops into sugar mixture. Bake at 375 degrees for 8 to 10 minutes, watching carefully so sugar doesn't burn. Remove from oven. Mix powdered sugar, orange juice and remaining zest; brush glaze over warm knots. Let cool for 3 minutes and serve. Serves 4 to 6.

Java Chiller

*Crystal Shook
Catawba, NC*

*A great way to use leftover coffee...perfect for sipping on
a hot summer day!*

4 c. cold brewed coffee
3/4 to 1 c. favorite flavored liquid
   coffee creamer

4 c. crushed ice
Garnish: whipped cream,
   chocolate or caramel syrup

In a pitcher, combine all ingredients except garnish; stir until mixed well. Divide among 4 tall glasses. Top with whipped cream; garnish with a drizzle of syrup. Makes 4 servings.

Freeze extra coffee in ice cube trays...perfect for cooling a tall glass of iced coffee.

Spring & Summer
Recipes for Sharing

Grandma's Crunchies

Diana Krol
Hutchinson, KS

I've been making variations of this granola recipe for years. I especially like to make it in the summertime, when I prefer a simple breakfast or snack. It originated many years ago with my 4-H food leader. She was a wonderful cook and such an inspiration to me. Enjoy with milk or yogurt, or sprinkled over ice cream.

8 c. old-fashioned oats, uncooked
1 c. whole-wheat flour
1 c. cornmeal
1 c. sugar
1 c. wheat bran
1/2 c. wheat germ
7-oz. pkg. flaked coconut

10-oz. pkg. unsalted sunflower kernels
1 t. salt
1/2 c. butter, melted
1/4 c. water
1/2 c. honey or molasses
1 T. vanilla extract

In a large bowl, combine oats, flour, cornmeal, sugar, wheat bran, wheat germ, coconut, sunflower kernels and salt; toss to mix and set aside. In a separate bowl, stir together remaining ingredients; add to oat mixture. Mix well and spread mixture evenly in an ungreased roasting pan or large rimmed baking sheet. Bake, uncovered, at 275 degrees for one hour, stirring every 15 minutes, until toasted and golden. Remove from oven and cool. Store in a tightly covered container. Serves 20.

Optional add-ins: Before baking, stir in one cup coarsely chopped walnuts, 1/2 cup sesame seed or flax seed or one tablespoon cinnamon. After baking, stir in one cup chopped dried apricots, mixed dried fruit, dried cranberries or raisins.

Save the plastic liners when you toss out empty cereal boxes.
They're perfect for storing homemade granola.

Fresh-Picked
Salads

Spring & Summer
Recipes for Sharing

Nichole's Italian Salad

Nichole Hawkins
Decatur, IN

This salad tastes like it comes from a restaurant and is requested everywhere I go. It's great for church gatherings, family and school events. Be sure to bring extra recipe cards along to pass out, since you're sure to get requests!

1 head iceberg lettuce, chopped
1 to 2 bunches green onions,
   chopped
8-oz. pkg. shredded mozzarella
   cheese

1 c. shredded Parmesan cheese
5-oz. pkg. cheese & garlic
   croutons

In a large container with a lid, combine lettuce, onions and cheeses. Add lid; shake container to mix well. Chill until serving time. Just before serving, drizzle Dressing over salad. Cover again; shake very well to coat evenly. Top with croutons and serve. Makes 8 to 10 servings.

Dressing:

1 c. canola oil
1/2 c. cider vinegar
1/2 to 3/4 c. sugar, to taste
2 T. Italian salad dressing mix

2 T. cornstarch
2 t. garlic powder
1 t. salt

Whisk together all ingredients; transfer to a covered container and refrigerate.

Fresh-Picked
Salads

Maegan's Garden Salad

Maegan Stauffer
Findlay, OH

*We love fresh veggies in the hot Ohio summer months! My daughter
is allergic to tomatoes, so this recipe is a good choice for her.*

5-1/2 c. broccoli, finely chopped
2 c. cauliflower, finely chopped
2 c. baby carrots, sliced
4-oz. block medium Cheddar
   cheese, diced

1 c. light mayonnaise
1/2 c. large-curd cottage cheese
1 T. sugar
1 T. bread-and-butter pickle juice
1/2 t. dried, minced onions

Combine broccoli, cauliflower and carrots in a large bowl; set aside.
Combine remaining ingredients in a small bowl; add to broccoli mixture.
Toss to coat well. Cover and refrigerate for 6 hours to overnight and
serve. Makes 8 to 10 servings.

On the kids' last day of school, serve an all-finger-food
dinner just for fun. Serve chicken nuggets, French fries and
fresh carrot and celery dippers with cups of creamy ranch
dressing. For dessert, frosty fruit pops or ice cream
sandwiches are perfect. Pass the napkins, please!

Spring & Summer
Recipes for Sharing

Thunder & Lightening Salad

Marsha Pounds
Rolla, MO

This recipe was given to me by a neighbor in Indiana about 40 years ago. Served chilled, it is very refreshing as part of a summer meal.

3 ripe tomatoes, cubed
3 green or red peppers, cubed
1 large onion, cubed
2 banana peppers, diced

1 hot pepper, diced
1/2 c. celery, diced
3 T. white vinegar
salt and pepper to taste

Combine all vegetables in a large bowl. Add vinegar, salt and pepper; mix well. Cover and chill; serve cold. Makes 6 servings.

Ranch Cherry Tomatoes

Pam Hooley
LaGrange, IN

This is best in the summertime, with garden-ripe tomatoes and fresh basil. Goes together fast, and you can set it aside to blend flavors while you make the rest of the meal.

3 c. cherry tomatoes, halved
salt and pepper to taste
2/3 c. buttermilk
3 T. fresh basil, sliced

1 shallot or 2 T. green onions,
  chopped
2 cloves garlic, minced

Add tomatoes to a bowl. Season with salt and pepper; set aside. In another bowl, stir together remaining ingredients; pour over tomatoes. Let stand at room temperature up to one hour to allow flavors to blend. Serves 4 to 6.

Set out stacks of colorful bandannas...they make super-size
fun napkins when enjoying picnic foods.

Fresh-Picked
Salads

Bocconcini & Tomato Antipasto

Kathy Collins
Brookfield, CT

My family loves this quick, summery-looking salad.
I could eat it all the time!

3 c. red cherry tomatoes, halved
3 c. yellow grape tomatoes, halved
12 bocconcini fresh mozzarella cheese balls
1/4 c. fresh basil, finely chopped
1/2 c. extra-virgin olive oil
2 T. balsamic vinegar
1/4 t. salt
1/2 t. pepper

In a large bowl, combine tomatoes, cheese and basil; set aside. In a small bowl, whisk together remaining ingredients. Add to tomato mixture; toss gently to coat well. Serve immediately. Makes 8 servings.

Pesto Pasta Salad

Kristy Jensen
Williamsburg, VA

My husband and I came up with this recipe together. We both wanted a chilled pasta salad that was a little different. I had a jar of pesto sauce on hand and voilà, this creation was made. We both ate it for several days for lunch...so good!

16-oz. pkg. rotini pasta, uncooked
1/2 c. jarred pesto sauce
3/4 c. creamy Italian salad dressing
3/4 c. grated Parmesan cheese

Cook pasta according to package directions; drain. Rinse with cold water and drain; transfer to a large bowl. Add pesto sauce, salad dressing and cheese; mix well. Cover and refrigerate for 4 hours or overnight. Serves 10 to 12.

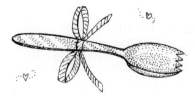

The serrated edges of a grapefruit spoon make
quick work of hulling tomatoes.

Spring & Summer
Recipes for Sharing

Penne & Prosciutto Salad

Sharon Winters
Anderson, SC

When I needed a recipe for a potluck dish, my friend gave me this one. I made it and afterwards, there was none left. I also made it for a family Christmas party, using pasta in holiday shapes. Again, no leftovers!

16-oz. pkg. penne pasta,
    uncooked
1 lb. sugar snap peas, trimmed
1 orange pepper, diced
1/2 c. onion, chopped
14-oz. can artichoke hearts,
    drained

1 c. pitted Kalamata olives,
    drained
1/4 lb. thin-sliced prosciutto,
    cut into 1/2-inch strips
1/2 c. grated Parmesan cheese

Cook pasta according to package directions; drain. Rinse with cold water and drain. Meanwhile, add peas to a saucepan of boiling water. Boil for 3 to 4 minutes; drain. Add peas to a bowl of ice water; drain. In a large bowl, combine pasta, peas and remaining ingredients. Drizzle with Oregano Dressing; toss to coat well. Cover and chill before serving. Makes 8 servings.

Oregano Dressing:

1/4 c. olive oil
1/4 c. red wine vinegar
1/2 t. salt

1/2 t. pepper
1/4 c. fresh oregano, chopped

Whisk together all ingredients.

Bring out Mom's cheery fruit
and flower table linens for
special family get-togethers.
Sure to spark conversations
about other special gatherings
through the years!

Fresh-Picked Salads

Butter Bean Delight

Debbie Ucci
Waco, TX

I have loved butter beans since I was a little girl. Whenever a pot of butter beans is fixed, there are always leftovers to use in this salad, but now it's so easy to open a couple of cans to make it. Great for picnics, as none of the ingredients spoils easily.

2 16-oz. cans butter beans,
    drained, or 3 c. cooked
    butter beans
15-1/4 oz. can corn, drained
2 c. grape tomatoes, halved or
    quartered

1 cucumber, peeled and
    finely diced
1/2 c. red onion, finely diced
1/2 to 1 c. fresh cilantro, to taste,
    coarsely chopped

Combine all ingredients in a large salad bowl; toss to mix well. Add Lime Dressing; toss again. Cover and chill for about 4 hours to allow flavors to blend. Toss again at serving time. Serves 8.

Lime Dressing:

1/2 c. olive oil or avocado oil
1-1/2 T. lime juice
1 t. garlic, finely minced
1/2 t. ground cumin

salt to taste
2 t. pepper
1/4 t. cayenne pepper

Whisk together all ingredients.

It's a challenge to keep foods chilled on a hot, sunny day when everyone is opening and closing the cooler to get cold drinks. Make it easy...pack one cooler with beverages and another with meats, salads and other perishable foods.

Spring & Summer
Recipes for Sharing

Grilled Romaine Salad

Bethany Scott
Huntsville, AL

Grilling lettuce makes it smoky-tasting and delicious. Give it a try with different dressings...it's good with Green Goddess and Greek salad dressing, too.

3 to 4 heads romaine lettuce, trimmed and outer leaves removed
1 small red onion, cut into 6 to 8 thin wedges

2 T. olive oil
buttermilk salad dressing to taste
salt and pepper to taste
Garnish: shredded Parmesan cheese

Cut romaine lettuce heads in half lengthwise, keeping heads intact. Brush lettuce and onion evenly with olive oil. Spray grill with non-stick vegetable spray; arrange onion wedges on grill over medium heat. Cover and grill for 3 to 4 minutes on each side. Remove onion; set aside. Place lettuce halves cut-side down on grill. Grill, uncovered, for one to 2 minutes, just until lettuce is wilted. Divide grilled lettuce evenly among 6 to 8 salad plates, cut-side up. Top each with one onion wedge, separated into slices; drizzle with salad dressing. Season with salt and pepper; add a sprinkle of cheese and serve immediately. Serves 6 to 8.

Whip up a side dish in no time at all...layer thick slices of juicy tomatoes with fresh mozzarella cheese, then drizzle with olive oil. Sprinkle with fresh basil and serve.

Fresh-Picked
Salads

Italian Pasta Salad

LaDeana Cooper
Batavia, OH

My late stepfather introduced me to the original recipe for this salad. I have made a few changes to better suit my taste, and it's perfect for barbecues and picnics. Add your favorite garden veggies...blanched green beans, sliced carrots and Brussels sprouts are all good. You can even replace the pasta with spiralized, uncooked zucchini or yellow squash.

12-oz. pkg. bowtie or other
   favorite pasta, uncooked
1 pt. grape or cherry tomatoes,
   halved
2 c. assorted green, red,
   orange and yellow peppers,
   finely diced

1/2 c. red onion, finely diced
8-oz. can sliced black olives,
   drained
zesty Italian salad dressing
   to taste

Cook pasta according to package directions; drain. Rinse with cold water and drain; place pasta in a large bowl. Add remaining ingredients except salad dressing. Add just enough dressing to coat; toss to mix. Cover and and refrigerate. The longer salad is refrigerated, the more the flavors will blend. Makes 10 or more servings.

Welcome a new neighbor with a basket filled with the flavors of summer...ripe tomatoes, cucumbers, sweet corn and an invitation to come along, next time you visit the farmers' market.

Spring & Summer
Recipes for Sharing

Healthy 3-Bean Salad

Gladys Kielar
Whitehouse, OH

Some ladies have cookie exchange parties...one summer, my friends and I had a salad get-together party! We each made our favorite salad recipe for everyone to taste, with copies of the recipe to take home. We all took home 20 new salad recipes. It was such a hit, we planned to get together and do it again with soup recipes.

15-1/2 oz. can kidney beans
14-1/2 oz. can French-style
   green beans
14-1/2 oz. can yellow wax beans
1/2 c. onion, chopped

8-oz. bottle Italian salad dressing
1 T. sugar
2 cloves garlic, minced
Garnish: crisp lettuce leaves

Add all beans to a colander and drain. Rinse well; drain again. In a large bowl with a tight-fitting lid, combine all beans and onion; set aside. In a small bowl, stir together salad dressing, sugar and garlic. Pour over bean mixture and toss. Cover and refrigerate at least 3 hours, stirring occasionally. Just before serving, remove bean mixture with a slotted spoon to a lettuce-lined salad bowl. Makes 6 servings.

Trim a big canvas tote bag with quilt squares, attached with
simple stitching or fabric glue. So handy for carrying
home goodies from the farmers' market!

Fresh-Picked Salads

Summer Squash Salad

Denise Webb
Bloomingdale, GA

I tasted this salad at a picnic and enjoyed it very much. It's a great way to showcase yellow squash and zucchini from your garden.

2 small yellow squash,
   coarsely chopped
2 small zucchini, coarsely
   chopped
1/2 c. red pepper, diced
1/3 c. red onion, sliced
2 T. cider vinegar or
   red wine vinegar

3 T. oil
1 T. mayonnaise
1 t. sugar
1/2 t. dill weed
1/2 t. garlic salt
1/4 t. celery salt
1/4 t. pepper

Combine all vegetables in a large bowl; set aside. In a small bowl, whisk together remaining ingredients; mix well. Pour over squash mixture and toss to coat. Cover and refrigerate. Serve with a slotted spoon. Makes 6 to 8 servings.

Mamaw's Easy Coleslaw

Jimmy Cox
Westfield, IN

I never used to like coleslaw until I tried my mamaw's version. Made by her daughter, who was my grandma, this version is finely chopped and similar to a famous take-out version, but much better. I remember having it the first time as a late-night snack when I was looking through the fridge. Now I make it every spring and summer. The key is to use the best mayonnaise. Every time I make it, I think of my mamaw and grandma.

1 large or 2 small heads cabbage,
   finely chopped
1 sweet onion, finely chopped

1/4 c. carrot, finely chopped
2 c. mayonnaise
1/4 c. sugar, divided

In a large bowl, combine all vegetables. Add mayonnaise; mix together well. Sprinkle with half of sugar and mix; sprinkle with remaining sugar and mix. Cover and refrigerate at least 4 hours. At serving time, mix again and serve. Serves 15.

Spring & Summer
Recipes for Sharing

Mediterranean Chickpea Salad

Karen Antonides
Gahanna, OH

This healthy salad provides vegetables and plant-based protein in a fresh, delicious salad. My daughter is a vegetarian, so I enjoy trying to find recipes that she will enjoy.

1/2 c. extra-virgin olive oil
1/4 c. red wine vinegar
salt and pepper to taste
2 15-oz. cans chickpeas, drained
   and rinsed
1 pt. cherry tomatoes, sliced

1 small cucumber, diced
1/2 c. crumbled feta cheese
1/2 c. pitted Kalamata olives,
   sliced
1/4 c. fresh parsley, chopped
1/4 c. fresh mint, chopped

In a small bowl, whisk together oil, vinegar, salt and pepper; set aside. In a large bowl, combine remaining ingredients. Add oil mixture and toss together well. Cover and chill until serving time. Makes 8 servings.

Add a little springtime whimsy to a buffet table...under an old-fashioned glass garden cloche, arrange a little bird's nest and a tiny bluebird from a craft store.

Fresh-Picked
Salads

Greek Orzo Salad

Andrea Czarniecki
Northville, MI

This is a quick & easy salad to round out any summer lunch or dinner.

16-oz. pkg. orzo pasta, uncooked
1 green pepper, diced
1 red pepper, diced
1 yellow pepper, diced
1 cucumber, peeled and diced
1/2 red onion, diced
1 c. sliced black olives, drained

15-1/2 oz. can black beans, drained
Optional: crumbled feta cheese to taste
zesty Italian salad dressing to taste

Cook pasta according to package directions; drain. Rinse with cold water; drain again and transfer to a large bowl. Add all vegetables, olives, beans and cheese, if using. Toss with salad dressing to taste. Cover and chill at least one hour; the longer it chills, the more intense the flavor will be. Makes 6 to 8 servings.

Turkish Salad

Lori Crawford
Glen Allen, VA

A fresh-tasting salad I learned to make when living overseas. I've adapted the recipe a bit over the years. It's served at room temperature, so it's great for potlucks.

8 to 10 roma tomatoes, cubed
3 medium cucumbers, cubed
4 green onions, sliced

3 T. extra-virgin olive oil
1 t. dried basil
1 to 2 t. salt, to taste

Combine all vegetables in a large non-metallic bowl. Add olive oil and basil; toss together until thoroughly mixed. Season with salt; mix well. Cover and refrigerate for at least one hour. Serve at room temperature using a slotted spoon. Makes 12 servings.

Spring & Summer
Recipes for Sharing

Mexican Cobb Salad

Carol Reffner
Upland, CA

*I served this salad at my daughter's baby shower. It's perfect
for a light summer meal...great for potlucks, too!*

2 c. grilled chicken breasts,
   cut into chunks
1/2 head iceberg lettuce, torn
1 avocado, peeled, pitted and
   cut into 1-inch cubes
1 ripe tomato, chopped
1 c. shredded Cheddar cheese
1 c. celery, sliced

1/2 c. green onions, chopped
1/2 c. carrot, peeled and grated
1/2 c. canned kidney beans,
   drained and rinsed
1/2 c. buttermilk salad dressing
4-oz. pkg. tortilla chips, lightly
   crushed

In a large bowl, combine all ingredients except salad dressing and
tortilla chips. Toss to mix; cover and refrigerate until ready to serve. At
serving time, toss with salad dressing and top with crushed chips. Serve
immediately. Makes 6 servings.

Keep a basket of picnic supplies in your car for picnics at
a moment's notice! With a quilt or tablecloth, paper napkins,
plates and cups you'll always be ready. Just pick up sandwich
fixin's and drinks and you're ready to go!

Fresh-Picked
Salads

Tomato Bread Salad

Lisa Ashton
Aston, PA

My mom used to find creative ways to use up the tomatoes from my father's garden. A bread salad is a great summertime meal!

4 c. ripe tomatoes, diced
3/4 c. red onion, sliced
1/2 c. water
1/3 c. olive oil
1/3 c. white wine vinegar
1 t. sugar
1 t. salt
1 t. pepper
1/2 c. fresh basil, shredded
6 c. day-old bread, cut into
   1-inch cubes

In a large bowl, combine all ingredients except bread cubes. Toss to mix well; let stand about 15 minutes. Add bread cubes; toss well to coat and serve. Salad will hold at room temperature up to 2 hours. Serves 6.

We grew up in the Ozark Hills along the Buffalo National River, which is surrounded by creeks and steep hillsides. When it was July-hot here in Arkansas in the early to mid-1970s, air conditioning was not common. Many evenings after Mom got home from work, we would all load up in the back of Dad's pickup truck, taking only a cast-iron skillet, lard and a bucket of potatoes, plus a frozen milk jug of fruit punch or water, and cook on the river bank. We'd swim while a pan of potatoes fried...usually we'd enjoy them with sliced home-grown tomatoes. Fried potatoes never tasted so good! Mom didn't have to heat up the kitchen and we didn't have to take baths after we got home. On really special days, we had juicy watermelon also. Wonderful memories!

–Pam Massey, Marshall, AR

Spring & Summer
Recipes for Sharing

Cranberry Pecan Slaw

Barbara Bargdill
Gooseberry Patch

This is a quick & easy salad for summer that's just a little different. I use a lighter, healthier coleslaw dressing to keep it light. It makes a lot, so we sometimes enjoy it as a main dish with some good hearty country-style bread.

32-oz. pkg. shredded
  coleslaw mix
2 Fuji or Honeycrisp apples,
  cored and chopped
1-1/2 c. dried cranberries

1-1/2 c. salted pecans, chopped
1 bunch green onions, sliced
favorite coleslaw dressing
  to taste

In a large bowl, combine all ingredients except salad dressing; toss to mix. Add coleslaw dressing to taste; toss until mixed well. Serve immediately, or cover and refrigerate until ready to serve. Toss again lightly, adding more dressing if needed. Makes 8 servings.

4th of July Salad

Marcia Shaffer
Conneaut Lake, PA

On the 4th of July, the peaches are always full on the trees, fragrant and rosy. Here is a great summer gelatin salad that is sure to become a tradition. Very pretty!

3-oz. pkg. peach gelatin mix
1 c. boiling water
3/4 c. cold water
1 c. ripe peaches, peeled, pitted
  and sliced

1/2 c. blueberries
1/4 c. honeydew melon, sliced
1/4 c. seedless grapes
sliced lettuce leaves

In a bowl, combine gelatin mix and boiling water; stir until gelatin is dissolved. Stir in cold water. Pour into a 13"x9" glass baking pan. Cover and refrigerate for about 4 hours, until gelatin begins to thicken. Gently blend in fruits, distributing evenly throughout gelatin. Refrigerate several hours, or overnight, until firm. Cut into squares; serve on lettuce leaves. Serves 6.

Fresh-Picked
Salads

Red, White & Blue Summer Salad *Vivian Marshall*
Columbus, OH

This quick & easy salad is always a grand slam. It's so refreshing, and goes great with burgers on the grill! It's one of our favorite summer salads, and there are rarely leftovers. Just for fun, I like to serve the salad out of the empty watermelon shell! It's beautiful on the table. Be sure to slice a bit off of the bottom so it sits flat.

1/2 of a round seedless
   watermelon, cut into
   bite-size cubes or balls
1-1/2 c. fresh blueberries

5-oz. container crumbled
   feta cheese
Optional: chopped fresh
   mint leaves

Gently toss all ingredients together in a large bowl. Serve immediately, or cover and refrigerate until serving time. The more chilled, the better! Makes 4 to 6 servings.

Strawberry-Orange Pasta Salad *Maureen Charnigo*
Medina, OH

I found this recipe years ago in a cooking magazine. Whenever I take it, people want the recipe, so I have learned to always make a double batch!

2 c. bowtie pasta, uncooked
1/3 c. creamy poppy seed
   dressing
1/4 c. mayonnaise
4 green onions, sliced

11-oz. can mandarin oranges,
   drained
1 c. fresh strawberries, hulled
   and sliced

Cook pasta as directed on package; drain. Rinse with cool water; drain. Meanwhile, mix together salad dressing and mayonnaise in a large bowl. Add cooked pasta and onions; toss to coat. Gently stir in fruit. Cover and refrigerate for one hour. Makes 4 servings.

Spring & Summer
Recipes for Sharing

Greek Quinoa Salad

Lisa Ann Panzino DiNunzio
Vineland, NJ

Hearty, healthy, tasty!

2 c. cooked quinoa, cooled
1/2 c. pitted Kalamata olives
1/2 c. onion, diced
1 c. cherry tomatoes, halved

1/2 English cucumber, peeled
    and diced
1/2 c. crumbled feta cheese

Rinse cooked quinoa with cold water; drain and transfer to a large bowl. Add olives, onion, tomatoes and cucumber. Add Lemony Dressing; gently toss all together. Add feta cheese; toss once more. Cover and refrigerate for at least one hour. Toss again before serving. Makes 4 to 6 servings.

Lemony Dressing:

1/4 c. extra-virgin olive oil
    to taste
1 T. cider vinegar or balsamic
    vinegar to taste

juice of one lemon
1/2 t. dried oregano
sea salt and pepper to taste

Combine all ingredients; whisk well.

Setting out picnic food? Remember...safety first!
Keep hot foods hot, cold foods cold, and don't let
any picnic foods stand out longer than 2 hours.

Fresh-Picked
Salads

Jicama Salad

Bev Traxler
British Columbia, Canada

*Jicama (pronounced hick-ah-mah) salad is crunchy
and refreshing...a great addition to any meal.*

1 large jicama, peeled and cut
   into thin matchsticks
1/2 green pepper, finely diced
1/2 red pepper, finely diced
1/2 yellow pepper, finely diced
1/2 cucumber, seeded and
   chopped
1/2 c. red onion, diced

1 navel orange, peeled
   and chopped
1/2 c. fresh cilantro, chopped
1/2 c. lime juice
1/8 t. cayenne pepper
1/8 t. paprika
salt to taste

Toss together jicama, peppers, cucumber, onion, orange and cilantro
in a large bowl. Drizzle lime juice over all. Sprinkle with cayenne and
paprika; season generously with salt. Let stand at room temperature for
30 minutes before serving. Makes 4 servings.

Happiness is to hold flowers in both hands.
–Japanese proverb

Spring & Summer
Recipes for Sharing

Grandma's Shrimp Potato Salad

Julie Hutson
Callahan, FL

This delicate salad always reminds me of warm, summer Saturday afternoons at my grandparents' home. My grandma cooked everyday. She always made a big breakfast and then cooked the traditional Southern "dinner" to be served mid-afternoon. This special salad always takes me right back to her kitchen table...sweet and delicious memories!

6 potatoes, peeled and cut into
    small cubes
1 lb. cooked shrimp, peeled
    and chopped
1 stalk celery, chopped fine

1/2 c. mayonnaise
salt to taste
Optional: crisply cooked,
    crumbled bacon

Cook potatoes in a saucepan of salted, boiling water until fork-tender; drain well. Transfer to a large bowl; very lightly mash some of the potatoes. Add remaining ingredients and gently stir to blend. Cover and chill until serving time. Makes 6 servings.

Remember that happy feeling you had as a kid when a party invitation arrived in the mail? Whether it's a baby shower or a backyard cookout, send out written invitations...friends will love it!

Fresh-Picked
Salads

Tuna Celery Salad

Joanne Mauseth
Clear Lake, SD

Growing up in our old house on the farm, we had no air conditioning and sometimes the summers could get so hot and humid. Mom would make this salad for us on evenings when it was too hot to cook. It was cool and filling. It goes great with wedges of juicy, ripe cantaloupe for dessert.

2 6-oz. cans tuna, drained
   and flaked
1 bunch celery, chopped

1/4 c. onion, finely diced
1/2 c. mayonnaise
seasoned salt and pepper to taste

Combine tuna, celery and onion in a bowl; mix together. Stir in mayonnaise. For a creamier texture, add a little more mayonnaise or a little milk. Season with salt and pepper; cover and chill before serving. Makes 6 to 8 servings.

West Indies Crab Salad

Mary Donaldson
Enterprise, AL

When I first arrived in Pensacola, Florida in 1967, my neighbor shared this recipe with me. It's still one of my all-time favorites.

3/4 c. onion, finely chopped
   and divided
1 lb. fresh lump crabmeat, flaked
salt and pepper to taste

1/2 c. oil
6 T. cider vinegar
1/2 c. ice water

Spread half of onion in the bottom of a large bowl; cover with crabmeat. Add remaining onion, salt and pepper; set aside. In a small bowl, stir together oil, vinegar and ice water; pour over crabmeat mixture. Cover and marinate for 2 to 12 hours. Toss lightly before serving. Makes 4 servings.

Keep salads chilled...simply nestle the salad bowl
into a larger bowl filled with crushed ice.

Spring & Summer
Recipes for Sharing

Coleslaw Chicken Salad

Nancy Putnam
Lake Stevens, WA

My longtime favorite summertime salad! My mother-in-law made this very often and it has many special memories for me. It goes well with burgers on the grill.

1/2 c. sliced almonds
2 T. sesame seed
4 boneless, skinless chicken
   breasts, cooked and cubed
1 head cabbage, chopped

4 green onions, chopped
3-oz. pkg. ramen noodles,
   uncooked and broken
   into pieces

Heat a skillet over medium-high heat; add almonds and sesame seed. Cook and stir for several minutes until toasted, watching carefully; cool. In a large bowl, combine chicken, almonds and sesame seed. Add cabbage, onions and noodles; reserve ramen seasoning packet for another use. Toss to mix; cover and chill. Just before serving, pour Cider Vinegar Dressing over salad; toss well and serve. Makes 6 to 8 servings.

Cider Vinegar Dressing:

1/2 c. oil
3 T. cider vinegar
2 T. sugar

1 t. powdered flavor enhancer
1 t. salt
1/2 t. pepper

Combine all ingredients in a covered container; shake well.

Tuck leftover chopped salad into pita rounds for
a quick, tasty lunch.

Fresh-Picked
Salads

Grandma Stadelman's Penne Salad

Peter Stadelman
Williamsville, NY

I found this recipe when my dad was cleaning out his office. I made this salad for a picnic with my fiancée and we just loved it. Hope it becomes a summer tradition for you too!

16-oz. pkg. penne pasta,
    uncooked
4 t. white vinegar
1 T. salad oil
2 t. sugar
2 T. mustard
1 T. dried parsley
1 t. garlic powder
1/4 t. celery seed
1/4 t. dill weed
1 t. salt
1 t. pepper
4-oz. jar sliced pimentos,
    drained
1 onion, diced
1 cucumber, diced

Cook pasta according to package directions, drain. Rinse with cold water; drain again and add to a large bowl. Add vinegar, oil, sugar and seasonings; toss to coat pasta well. Add pimentos, onion and cucumber. Cover and refrigerate for several hours to overnight before serving. Makes 8 to 10 servings.

Keep flying insects out of picnic beverages! Stitch 4 large beads or pretty seashells to the corners of a table napkin and drape over the open pitcher.

Spring Spinach Salad

Emily Doody
Kentwood, MI

This salad with its warm bacon dressing is a show-stopper! It's perfect for a cookout, paired with grilled chicken or fish. I especially love it when spring is just peeking in and I am craving something fresh. You can even add fresh strawberries to really brighten things up. Enjoy with a basket of hot rolls.

1/2 lb. sliced bacon
6-oz. pkg. baby spinach
1 cucumber, halved and sliced
4-oz. log goat cheese, crumbled
3 eggs, hard-boiled, peeled and chopped
1/2 red onion, cut into matchsticks and divided

1/4 c. olive oil
salt, pepper and red pepper flakes to taste
1/2 c. cider vinegar
1 T. maple syrup

Cook bacon in a skillet over medium heat until crisp. Remove bacon to paper towels to drain. Pour off excess drippings from skillet. Do not wipe out skillet; set aside. In a large bowl, toss together spinach, cucumber, cheese, eggs and crumbled bacon. Add 2 tablespoons onion matchsticks to spinach mixture; set aside. Finely chop remaining onion; add to drippings in skillet along with olive oil and seasonings. Sauté over medium heat until onion is soft and golden. Add vinegar and syrup; cook for another 2 minutes. Pour hot dressing from skillet over salad; toss and serve. Makes 6 to 8 servings.

Hosting a baby shower? Ask guests to each bring a baby photo.
The first person to guess who's who gets a prize!

Fresh-Picked
Salads

Summer Potato Salad

Kay Daugherty
Collinsville, MS

My family adores this recipe and I make it every July 4th. You can use your favorite bottled ranch salad dressing, but I always make mine fresh with the ranch packet. You will be amazed by the flavor of this salad!

2 lbs. new redskin potatoes
1 head broccoli, cut into
    bite-size flowerets
salt and pepper to taste
1-1/2 c. ranch salad dressing

Optional: 1 T. horseradish sauce
1/2 c. red onion, diced
3/4 lb. bacon, crisply cooked
    and crumbled

Add potatoes to a saucepan of boiling water; do not peel. Cook until fork-tender and drain. Cut potatoes into quarters; transfer to a large bowl. Add broccoli; season generously with salt and pepper. Set aside. In a small bowl, combine salad dressing and horseradish sauce, if using. Add onion and mix thoroughly. Drizzle salad dressing mixture over potato mixture; stir gently. For best flavor, cover and refrigerate overnight. At serving time, transfer to your prettiest salad bowl. Top with crumbled bacon and serve. Makes 6 to 8 servings.

Potatoes come in 3 basic types. Round waxy potatoes are excellent in soups, casseroles and potato salads. Starchy russet potatoes bake up fluffy...great for frying, too. All-purpose potatoes are in between and work well in most recipes. Do some delicious experimenting to find your favorites!

Spring & Summer
Recipes for Sharing

Oh-So-Easy Mason Jar Vinaigrette
Kristy Wells
Ocala, FL

We're always trying to fit in extra veggies! One dish my whole family enjoys eating is salad. I've been concocting my own dressings for years and they are very versatile, easily changing flavors just by using different vinegars. This is a summertime favorite of mine and I use it on bagged salad greens topped with sliced rotisserie chicken for a healthy, well-balanced meal. It can also be used as a marinade.

1 c. olive oil
1/2 c. cider vinegar
1/2 c. water
2 T. garlic, minced

1 T. Italian seasoning
1 T. honey
1/4 t. pepper

Combine all ingredients in a one-pint mason jar. Add lid securely and shake vigorously. Store in refrigerator for up to 2 weeks. Makes 6 to 8 servings.

Variations: Recipe may be altered by using different vinegars and seasonings, and by adding diced fruit such as peaches, strawberries and raspberries, sun-dried tomatoes, avocado and fresh ginger.

For a casual supper, set up a mini salad bar with all the fixin's
in a muffin tin...everyone can choose their favorites.

Fresh-Picked
Salads

Honey-Garlic Salad Dressing

Diane Hixon
Niceville, FL

This dressing tastes fabulous on any salad! We served it in the cafe I had many years ago. I was fortunate enough to know a friend who sold local honey.

2 c. mayonnaise
1/3 c. oil
1/4 c. buttermilk
1/4 c. sour cream
3 T. honey

1 T. lemon juice
1 T. white wine vinegar
1 clove garlic, minced
3/4 t. dry mustard

Combine all ingredients in a blender; process until blended. Serve immediately, or cover and chill for later. Makes 3-1/2 cups.

Favorite Catalina Salad Dressing

Karen Wald
Dalton, OH

This is a go-to recipe that I almost always have made up and ready in my refrigerator. Serve on mixed greens or any lettuce salad. My husband says it is his favorite dressing!

2 t. dried, chopped onions
1/2 c. sugar
1/2 t. salt
1 t. pepper

1/3. catsup
1/2 c. canola oil or olive oil
1/4 c. lemon juice

In a one-pint canning jar, combine all ingredients in order listed. Add jar lid and shake to mix well. Keep refrigerated. Makes 20 servings.

Freeze juice boxes or bottles when packing a cooler.
They'll help keep other foods cold and will still be
cool to drink when you're ready.

Spring & Summer
Recipes for Sharing

Penn Dutch Hot Bacon Dressing

Bethi Hendrickson
Danville, PA

Here in central Pennsylvania, hot bacon and dandelion suppers are a staple in springtime. This dressing is wonderful on dandelion greens, lettuce or even hot potatoes...it's just yummy!

1 lb. sliced bacon
3 T. all-purpose flour
2 eggs, beaten
3/4 c. sugar or 1/2 c. calorie-free
    powdered sweetener

1 c. milk
1 c. water
3/4 c. vinegar
1/8 t. pepper

In a skillet over medium heat, cook bacon until crisp. Drain bacon on paper towels. Reserve 2 teaspoons drippings; allow to cool slightly. To a blender, add eggs, reserved drippings and remaining ingredients. Process until well blended; pour into a saucepan. Add crumbled bacon; cook and stir over low heat until thickened. Serve hot. Makes 2 to 3 cups.

Today is the day when bold kites fly,
When cumulus clouds roar across the sky.
When robins return, when children cheer,
When light rain beckons spring to appear.

–Robert McCracken

Fresh-Picked
Salads

Honey Dressing for Fruit

Nancy Putnam
Lake Stevens, WA

*This dressing is sooo delicious! I love to use it
on just about any combination of fresh fruit.*

1/3 c. honey
1/4 c. orange juice
1/4 c. canola oil
1-1/2 t. poppy seed

1/2 t. lemon juice
1/4 t. mustard
1/4 t. salt

Combine all ingredients in a jar with a tight lid; cover and shake well.
Keeps refrigerated for about 2 weeks. Makes about one cup.

Strawberry Vinaigrette

Mary Hughes
Talladega, AL

*A luscious dressing for salad greens, toasted nuts and
sliced strawberries or oranges...summer in a salad bowl!*

1 c. strawberry preserves
1/4 c. balsamic vinegar
1/4 c. Dijon mustard

1/2 t. cayenne pepper
1/2 c. olive oil
1/2 c. water

In a bowl, whisk together preserves, vinegar, mustard and pepper
until well blended. Gradually whisk in olive oil, then water. Serve
immediately, or cover and refrigerate. Makes 2-1/2 cups.

Here's an old trick for softening unripe fruit. Simply place it
in a brown paper bag...it'll ripen in a jiffy!

63

Spring & Summer
Recipes for Sharing

Fruit Salad for a Crowd
Wanda Baughman-Hunsecker
Fayetteville, PA

This recipe was from my husband's beloved Aunt Helen. She made gallons of this salad for every family reunion. It's a pretty salad and everyone loves it. Variations can be used...try a different flavor, if you like. Make it your own with your favorite fruit also. Serve with a smile!

3 3-oz. pkgs. orange gelatin mix
4 envs. unflavored gelatin
4 c. boiling water
4 12-oz. cans orange soda, chilled
2 lbs. Jonagold or Red Delicious apples, quartered, cored and chopped

3 lbs. seedless red grapes, halved
3 lbs. seedless green grapes, halved
2 12-oz. cans mandarin oranges, drained
2 12-oz. cans peach chunks, drained

In a large bowl, combine both gelatins and boiling water. Stir until well dissolved. Pour into a 13"x9" glass baking pan sprayed with non-stick vegetable spray. Cover and refrigerate until firm. Meanwhile, pour soda into a large bowl or container with a lid. Add apples; stir gently to cover. Add remaining fruit; stir again. Cut gelatin into small bite-size pieces; add to fruit mixture. Chill for 2 to 3 hours. Makes one gallon.

Always a summer favorite...a watermelon half, filled with melon balls, blueberries, strawberries, sliced peaches and other fresh fruit. Toss with a little lemon juice and honey for a tempting treat.

Farmstand
Sides

Spring & Summer
Recipes for Sharing

Zesty Garlic String Beans

Kristy Wells
Ocala, FL

This recipe is very simple and versatile, and everyone loves it. The cooking method gives this dish a nutty flavor, without cooking out the freshness. My husband and I used to have gigantic gardens every year with a huge overflow of fresh veggies. We would give away tons of them, but always had so much to eat ourselves. Those days were full of so many memories of our children, family & friends working together to create something wonderful, from the hard work outdoors, to the cooking and the kitchen table.

2 T. butter
2 T. olive oil
2 T. garlic, minced

2 lbs. fresh green beans, snapped
salt and pepper to taste

In a large cast-iron Dutch oven with a lid, melt butter with olive oil and garlic over low heat. Add green beans; toss to coat. Cover and cook over medium-low heat to medium heat, tossing occasionally, until beans are crisp-tender and just a little caramelized. Makes 6 to 8 servings.

Don't hesitate to ask questions at roadside stands! Growers are eager to tell you how to choose the freshest, tastiest produce and how to prepare it for the best flavor.

Farmstand
Sides

Baked Mozzarella Tomatoes
Bethany Richter
Canby, MN

This is a favorite of mine in the summertime. I love fresh garden-grown tomatoes, and the leftovers are just as good as the first batch out of the oven! Often I will save cooking time by using a package of real bacon pieces. Sometimes I will add a tablespoonful of dried, minced onions instead of the chopped onion.

4 to 5 ripe tomatoes, sliced
   and divided
8 c. soft bread cubes
3 to 4 c. shredded mozzarella
   cheese, divided
4 slices bacon, crisply cooked
   and crumbled

1/2 c. butter, melted
2 eggs, beaten
1/2 t. dried oregano
1/2 t. garlic salt
Optional: 1/2 c. chopped celery,
   1/2 c. chopped onion

Layer half of tomato slices in a greased 13"x9" baking pan; set aside. In a large bowl, combine bread cubes, 2 cups cheese, crumbled bacon, butter, eggs, seasonings, celery and onion, if using. Mix well; spoon mixture over tomatoes. Top with remaining tomatoes; sprinkle with remaining cheese. Bake, uncovered, at 350 degrees for 30 minutes, or until heated through. Makes 9 to 12 servings.

Give a June bride & groom a picnic basket as a wedding gift. Filled with napkins, plates, flatware, glasses and gourmet goodies, a bow tied to the handle is all that's needed to top it off.

Spring & Summer
Recipes for Sharing

July 4th Potato Packets

Carolyn Deckard
Bedford, IN

My husband and I created these tasty potato packets to go with our July 4th hamburgers while camping. The best part is, he does all the grilling!

8 russet potatoes, peeled and
    cut into thin strips
6 carrots, peeled and cut into
    thin strips
2/3 c. red onion, chopped

1/4 c. butter, sliced
Optional: 1 t. salt
1/4 t. pepper
1 c. shredded Parmesan or
    Cheddar cheese

Divide potatoes, carrots and onion equally among 6 to 8 pieces of heavy-duty aluminum foil, each 18 inches by 12 inches. Dot with butter; sprinkle with salt if desired and pepper. Bring opposite short ends of foil together over vegetables; crimp all edges tightly. Grill, covered, over medium coals for 20 to 30 minutes, until potatoes are tender. Remove from grill; carefully open foil. Divide cheese among packages. Reseal foil and set aside for 5 minutes, or until cheese melts. Serves 6 to 8.

When making grilling packets, heavy-duty aluminum foil is the best choice. It won't tear, holding in all the delicious juices.

Farmstand
Sides

Skillet Mexican Corn

Georgia Muth
Penn Valley, CA

Mexican corn on the cob known as "elote" is popular at fairs and street vendors in my California hometown. This is a skillet version that goes well with barbecues or other summer meals. If fresh corn is not available, frozen corn works well.

2 T. mayonnaise
1 T. lime juice
1-1/2 t. chili powder
2 T. oil
4 ears sweet corn, kernels cut off

Optional: 1/4 c. fresh cilantro,
   chopped
3 T. cotija or feta cheese,
   crumbled

Whisk together mayonnaise, lime juice and chili powder in a bowl until well mixed; set aside. Heat oil in a large cast-iron skillet over medium-high heat. Add corn; cook for 5 minutes without stirring. Toss corn with a spatula and continue cooking for another 3 minutes, or until golden. Remove from heat. Add mayonnaise mixture; stir until evenly combined. Stir in cilantro, if using. Transfer to serving plates; sprinkle with cheese and serve. Serves 4 to 6.

Cheesy Butter for Corn on the Cob

Kathy Grashoff
Fort Wayne, IN

Try this delicious spread on your next ears of sweet corn!

1/2 c. butter, softened
1 T. grated Parmesan or
   Romano cheese

2 T. red onion, finely chopped
1/2 t. paprika
1/2 t. white pepper

Combine all ingredients in a small bowl; stir until well blended. Cover and chill for one hour up to 24 hours, to allow flavors to blend. Serve at room temperature. Makes about 1/2 cup.

Spring & Summer
Recipes for Sharing

Grilled Vegetable Kabobs

Edward Kielar
Whitehouse, OH

You will love the marinade for these kabobs...give it a try!

4 to 6 bamboo skewers
2 to 3 redskin potatoes, cut into
   1-1/2 inch chunks
1 t. water

14 cherry tomatoes
1 zucchini, sliced 1/4-inch thick
1 yellow pepper, cut into
   one-inch chunks

Prepare Marinade; set aside. Meanwhile, soak skewers in water; drain.
Place potatoes in a microwave-safe bowl; sprinkle with water. Cover
and microwave for 3 to 4 minutes; drain. Alternately thread all
vegetables onto skewers. Grill kabobs, uncovered, over medium heat
for 8 to 10 minutes, until tender, brushing often with marinade. Makes
4 to 6 servings.

Marinade:

2 T. frozen orange juice
   concentrate
2 T. soy sauce
4-1/2 t. honey

1 t. oil
1/2 t. salt
1/8 t. red pepper flakes

Combine all ingredients in a bowl; mix well.

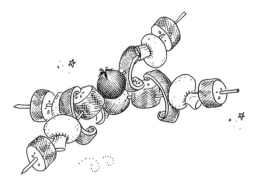

Make kabobs over a tabletop hibachi grill...so cozy
when it's just dinner for two.

Farmstand
Sides

Grammy's Baked Beans

Alicia Soncksen
Lincoln, NE

My husband's grandmother made this recipe for a family barbecue. It was an instant hit! I got the recipe from her and tweaked it slightly, and it still continues to be a hit at our family get-togethers. It's easy to make and serve in a slow cooker. Thanks, Grammy!

1 lb. ground beef
1/2 c. sweet onion, diced
1 lb. sliced turkey or pork bacon
2 28-oz. cans country-style
    baked beans

1 c. catsup
3/4 c. dark brown sugar, packed
1 T. chili powder
1 T. mustard

Brown beef with onion in a skillet over medium heat; drain and remove beef mixture from skillet. Wipe out skillet. Add bacon and cook until crisp; drain on paper towels. Transfer beef mixture and crumbled bacon to a 6-quart slow cooker. Add remaining ingredients; stir until well mixed. Cover and cook on low setting for 6 to 8 hours, or on high setting for 3 hours. Makes 16 servings.

Serve up frosty lemonade or iced tea with blueberry skewers.
Simply slide blueberries onto a wooden skewer until
covered; top with a fresh mint leaf...easy!

Zucchini Crescent Pie

Becky Kuchenbecker
Ravenna, OH

I've had this recipe for years, and every year it is the first thing I make with the fresh zucchini picked from our garden. Change it up with the cheese and herbs you add...don't be afraid to experiment!

8-oz. tube refrigerated crescent
  rolls, separated
1 to 2 T. mustard
1/2 c. butter
4 c. zucchini, thinly sliced
1 c. onion, chopped
2 eggs, beaten
1/2 c. fresh parsley, chopped,
  or 2 T. dried parsley

1/4 t. garlic powder
1/4 t. dried basil
1/4 t. dried oregano
1/2 t. salt
1/2 t. pepper
8-oz. pkg. shredded mozzarella
  cheese

Arrange crescent rolls in a 10" pie plate, forming a crust. Brush mustard over bottom and sides of crust; set aside. Combine butter, zucchini and onion in a skillet over medium heat; sauté for 10 minutes. Whisk together eggs, parsley, seasonings and cheese in a bowl; add to zucchini mixture in skillet. Mix well; spoon mixture into crust. Bake at 350 degrees for 15 minutes. Cover with aluminum foil; return to oven and bake another 10 minutes. Let stand for 10 minutes; cut into wedges and serve. Makes 8 servings.

And what is so rare as a day in June?
Then, if ever, come perfect days.

–James Russell Lowell

Farmstand Sides

Grandma's Southern Baked Mac & Cheese

Ann Davis
Brookville, IN

Grandma always had the most delicious food. This scrumptious macaroni & cheese is a must on picnic and potluck tables.

16-oz. pkg. elbow macaroni,
  uncooked
3 12-oz. cans evaporated milk
3 eggs, beaten
1-1/2 t. salt
1 t. pepper

1 t. dry mustard
1/8 t. cayenne pepper
3 8-oz. pkgs. shredded Cheddar
  cheese, divided
1/4 c. butter, sliced

Cook macaroni according to package directions; drain. In a large bowl, whisk together evaporated milk, eggs and seasonings. Spray a 3-quart casserole dish with non-stick vegetable spray. Layer half of cooked macaroni in dish; spread one package of cheese evenly over macaroni. Repeat layering; sprinkle evenly with remaining packages of cheese. Pour milk mixture evenly over all; dot with butter. Bake, uncovered, at 350 degrees for 40 to 45 minutes, until cheese is bubbly and lightly golden. Remove from oven; let stand 20 to 25 minutes before serving, to allow dish to set up. Makes 10 to 12 servings.

Traveling on vacation? Give your kids their own road maps... they can trace the route with markers and see how much farther you have to go.

Spring & Summer
Recipes for Sharing

Campfire Potatoes

Gladys Kielar
Whitehouse, OH

This side is great with any grilled main dish. You will love cooking it in aluminum foil...makes clean-up easy!

5 russet potatoes, peeled and
   thinly sliced
1 onion, sliced
6 T. butter, sliced
1/3 c. shredded Cheddar cheese

2 T. fresh parsley, minced
1 T. Worcestershire sauce
salt and pepper to taste
1/3 c. chicken broth

Spread potatoes and onion on a 20-inch square of heavy-duty aluminum foil; dot with butter. Combine cheese, parsley, Worcestershire sauce, salt and pepper; sprinkle over potatoes. Drizzle with chicken broth; fold foil up around potatoes. Tightly seal edges of foil; place package on a hot grill. Cover and grill over medium heat for 35 to 40 minutes, until potatoes are tender. Open package carefully. Makes 4 servings.

Fried Summer Squash

Anne Ptacnik
Holdrege, NE

My mom always raised a big garden, and yellow summer squash was a part of it every year. This simple recipe that she used could be depended on for hot, delicious results. Now that I raise my own garden, we make fried squash too...even the kids love it!

1 egg, beaten
salt and pepper to taste
1/2 c. all-purpose flour

1 to 2 yellow squash, sliced
   1/4-inch thick
3 T. butter, divided

Whisk together egg, salt and pepper in a shallow dish; place flour in another dish. Dip squash slices into egg mixture; dredge in flour. Melt half of butter in a skillet over medium heat. Add half of squash; cook on both sides until tender and golden. Remove to a plate; repeat with remaining butter and squash. Serves 4.

Farmstand
Sides

Loaded Cheese Fries

Karen Davis
Glendale, AZ

Great for cookouts and game-day parties...yummy!

26-oz. pkg. frozen crinkle-cut
  French fries
1-1/2 c. shredded sharp Cheddar
  cheese

6 slices bacon, crisply cooked
  and crumbled
Garnish: sour cream, sliced
  green onions

Cover a rimmed baking sheet with aluminum foil; spray with non-stick
vegetable spray. Spread frozen French fries evenly on pan. Bake at
425 degrees for 24 to 28 minutes, until crisp and golden. Top evenly
with cheese and bacon; bake another 3 to 5 minutes, until cheese is
melted. Serve garnished with sour cream and onions. Serves 10.

Baked Panko Parmesan Potatoes

Kimberly Redeker
Savoy, IL

A simple side, and a delicious one! The panko crumbs add
a nice crispness and make these potatoes memorable.

2 to 3 russet potatoes, peeled
  if desired and sliced
  1/4-inch thick
3 T. oil

1/4 c. panko bread crumbs
1/4 c. grated Parmesan cheese
1 T. garlic salt
1-1/2 t. pepper

Place potatoes in a large bowl. Drizzle with oil; stir to coat. Sprinkle
with remaining ingredients; mix again to coat. Spread on an aluminum
foil-lined rimmed baking sheet. Bake at 450 degrees for 18 to
25 minutes, until crisp and golden. Serves 4.

Serve French fries in tall paper cups, just like at the county fair!

Spring & Summer
Recipes for Sharing

Marsha's Summer Squash

Nan Wysock
New Port Richey, FL

A dear friend gave me this recipe years ago, after I fell in love with it when she served it one evening. Everyone I have made this dish for has loved it as well. It is simple and delicious.

3 lbs. yellow crookneck squash
   or summer squash, sliced
2 onions, sliced
3 eggs, beaten
1/2 c. butter, melted

2 T. sugar
1 c. chopped pecans
1 c. panko bread crumbs
Optional: shredded Parmesan
   cheese, sour cream

Combine squash and onions in a steamer pan over hot water. Cook over medium heat until squash is crisp-tender. Drain well; set aside in a bowl until cooled. Add remaining ingredients except pecans and bread crumbs; mix gently. Transfer to a greased 13"x9" baking pan; top with pecans and bread crumbs. Bake at 350 degrees for 30 minutes, until hot and bubbly. Top servings with a little Parmesan cheese and a dollop of sour cream, if desired. Makes 8 servings.

The pedigree of Honey
Does not concern the bee;
A clover, any time, to him
Is aristocracy.

–Emily Dickinson

Farmstand
Sides

Roasted Garlic Parmesan Cauliflower

Ann Farris
Biscoe, AR

This tasty recipe will have your kids eating cauliflower and asking for more. Hard to believe, I know!

1/2 c. butter, melted
2 cloves garlic, minced
1 c. Italian-flavored or plain
   dry bread crumbs
1/2 c. grated Parmesan cheese

1/4 t salt
1/4 t. pepper
1 head cauliflower, cut into
   bite-size flowerets

In a small bowl, combine melted butter and garlic. In another bowl, combine bread crumbs, cheese, salt and pepper. Dip each cauliflower floweret into butter, then into bread crumbs. Arrange on a lightly greased baking sheet. Bake at 400 degrees for 32 to 35 minutes, until tender and golden. Makes 6 servings.

Corn on the cob...perfect every time! Bring a stockpot of water to a boil and add corn. When the water returns to a boil, remove the stockpot from heat; cover and set the timer for 5 minutes.

Spring & Summer
Recipes for Sharing

Sesame Sweet Potato Packages

Lynda Hart
Bluffdale, UT

This is a wonderful side dish to serve with grilled chicken for a patio supper.

4 sweet potatoes, peeled and
    cut into 4 to 5 slices
1 to 2 T. oil
1 T. soy sauce

1 T. sesame seed
1 t. cinnamon
1/2 t. ginger
Garnish: chopped fresh parsley

Place sweet potato slices in a large bowl; add remaining ingredients except garnish. Toss until potatoes are well coated. Divide among 4 long pieces of aluminum foil. Crinkle foil up around potatoes and close tightly. Place packages on a hot grill and close the lid. Cook for 20 to 30 minutes, until tender. May also be baked at 350 degrees for 20 to 30 minutes. Open packages carefully; sprinkle with parsley and serve. Makes 4 servings.

Vintage tin pie plates are practical for serving meals when camping...not flimsy like paper plates! Look for tins that are stamped with the names of the original bakeries.

Farmstand
Sides

Michele's Baked Corn

Michele Shenk
Manheim, PA

I have been making this recipe since I was a newlywed, more than 30 years ago! Every year at our family reunion, a cousin would always ask me, "Did you bring your baked corn?" That was enough for me to keep bringing it year after year!

32-oz. pkg. frozen corn, thawed, or 4 c. fresh corn
2 T. butter, melted
2 T. sugar
2 T. all-purpose flour
1 t. salt
pepper to taste
2 eggs, well beaten
3/4 c. milk

In a large bowl, combine corn, butter, sugar, flour, salt and pepper; stir well. Add eggs and milk; stir again until well mixed. Spread evenly in a buttered 13"x9" baking pan. Bake, uncovered, at 350 degrees for 45 minutes, until heated through. Makes 6 to 8 servings.

4-Ingredient Hashbrown Bake

Beckie Apple
Grannis, AR

This recipe is so good and so easy, and it uses just four ingredients.

30-oz. pkg. frozen shredded hashbrown potatoes, thawed
2 10-3/4 oz. cans cream of chicken soup
16-oz. container sour cream
8-oz. pkg. shredded Cheddar cheese

Combine all ingredients in a large bowl; mix well. Spread evenly in a 13"x9" baking pan coated with non-stick vegetable spray. Bake, uncovered, at 350 degrees for 35 to 40 minutes, until bubbly and golden. Makes 6 to 8 servings.

A speedy, colorful side...sauté fresh green beans in
a little olive oil until crisp-tender and toss
with a jar of roasted red peppers.

Spring & Summer
Recipes for Sharing

Bacon & Onion Packet Potatoes

Sherry Lamb Noble
Paragould, AR

My dad came up with his version of this recipe in the 1960s. He loved to make dinner on the grill, and was always trying different food combinations cooked in foil on the grill. His bacon and onion potatoes were my favorite. Now, my family enjoys this side with grilled pork chops. It's a perfect side dish and so easy to make.

10 to 12 new redskin potatoes, thinly sliced
1/2 c. onion, diced
12 slices bacon, crisply cooked and crumbled
1.35-oz. pkg. onion soup mix
salt and pepper to taste
3 T. butter, sliced
Optional: 1 c. shredded Cheddar cheese
Garnish: sour cream

Spray 2 to 3 long pieces heavy-duty aluminum foil with non-stick vegetable spray. Divide potatoes, onion and bacon evenly among foil pieces. Sprinkle evenly with soup mix, salt and pepper. Dot with butter; top with cheese, if desired. Seal packages securely. Grill for 20 to 30 minutes. May also place packages on a baking sheet; bake at 350 degrees for about 35 minutes. Let stand for 10 minutes before opening. Serve in foil packages, topped with sour cream. Makes 6 servings.

Mix up a pitcher of frosty strawberry lemonade. Combine a 12-ounce can of frozen lemonade concentrate, a 10-ounce package of frozen strawberries and 4-1/2 cups of cold water. Let stand until the berries thaw and stir well. Wonderful!

Farmstand
Sides

Tomato-Bacon Pie

Jacki Smith
Fayetteville, NC

*This tasty pie is fresh and savory...a great way to enjoy
summer-ripe tomatoes! Fresh basil is the key. Perfect for
a summer luncheon or supper.*

9-inch pie crust, unbaked
2 to 3 ripe tomatoes, sliced and
   patted dry
1 T. fresh basil, chopped
6 slices bacon, crisply cooked
   and crumbled

salt and pepper to taste
1 c. mayonnaise
8-oz. pkg. shredded Cheddar
   Jack cheese
3 green onions, chopped

Arrange pie crust in a 9" pie plate. Bake at 350 degrees for 10 minutes;
remove from oven. Layer tomatoes, basil and bacon in crust; season
with salt and pepper. In a bowl, mix together mayonnaise and cheese;
spoon evenly over all. Sprinkle with onions. Bake at 350 degrees for
30 minutes, or until hot and bubbly. Let stand several minutes; cut into
wedges. Makes 6 servings.

Old-fashioned Mason jars make lovely lanterns for backyard
gatherings! Nestle a tea light inside and hang with wire from
tree branches or fenceposts. Look for citronella candles
to keep mosquitoes away.

Spring & Summer
Recipes for Sharing

Warm Summer Night Pasta

Kathryn Hinkle
Clinton, TN

This dish is good chilled or at room temperature. I like linguine pasta in it, but feel free to use your favorite. Cherry tomatoes, cut in half, can be used in place of larger tomatoes.

4 ripe tomatoes, cut into
   1/2-inch cubes
8 oil-packed sun-dried tomatoes,
   drained and cut into strips
8-oz. pkg. mozzarella cheese,
   cut into 1/2-inch cubes

1/2 c. fresh basil, cut into strips
1/4 c. extra-virgin olive oil, or
   more to taste
1 T. balsamic vinegar
16-oz. pkg. linguine pasta,
   uncooked

In a large bowl, combine all ingredients except pasta; mix well. Cover and refrigerate for 2 hours. Cook pasta according to package directions, just until tender; drain. Add cooked pasta to tomato mixture; toss to combine. Chill again, if desired. Makes 6 servings.

When chopping veggies, set the cutting board on
a damp kitchen towel and it won't slip.

Farmstand
Sides

Jill's Rice on the Grill

Jill Lovik
Naperville, IL

I have been making this recipe for 20 years, and my family always enjoys it! It's a handy recipe to have when you're grilling the rest of the meal. I use low-sodium broth and reduced-fat margarine.

1-1/3 c. instant rice, uncooked
1/4 c. green pepper, diced
1/4 c. onion, diced
1/2 c. chicken broth

1/2 c. water
1/3 c. catsup
1 T. butter, diced

Combine all ingredients except butter in a 9" aluminum foil pie plate; mix well. Dot with butter. Cover with heavy-duty foil; seal edges tightly. Grill, covered, for 14 to 15 minutes, until rice is tender and liquid is absorbed. Open carefully; fluff with a fork and serve immediately. Makes 6 servings.

Our garden consisted of tomatoes, squash, zucchini, green peppers, beets and kale. Mother also had onion sets in a barrel. In the summertime, there were so many tomatoes that she would can tomato juice in jars. She canned vegetables for vegetable soup in the wintertime, too. My grandmother would come from the country, bringing flat pole green beans. As they simmered, the delicious smell of green beans seasoned with bacon and whole potatoes drifted throughout the house. I'm so glad I have the sweet memories of my mother and grandmother. I miss the simpler life, but I'm so grateful and thankful for my summer memories.

–Patricia Taylor, Louisville, KY

Spring & Summer
Recipes for Sharing

Crispy Oven-Baked Green Bean Fries

Joyceann Dreibelbis
Wooster, OH

These crispy, crunchy green bean fries are baked in the oven, so they're a perfect healthy side dish. Pair them with your favorite veggie burger for an easy dinner!

3/4 lb. fresh green beans, ends trimmed
1 T. all-purpose flour
1 egg
3/4 c. panko bread crumbs

3 T. grated Parmesan cheese
1/2 t. salt
Optional: garlic powder and/or red pepper flakes to taste

In a large bowl, toss green beans with flour to coat lightly; set aside. Beat egg in a shallow bowl; combine panko crumbs, cheese, salt and desired seasonings in another bowl. Spray a baking sheet with non-stick vegetable spray. Dip beans into egg; coat with crumb mixture. Line green beans up in a single layer across pan. Bake at 425 degrees for 10 to 12 minutes, until coating is lightly golden. Makes 2 to 4 servings.

Use a damp sponge sprinkled with baking soda to scrub fruits and veggies, then rinse well. It works just as well as expensive cleansers for vegetables.

Farmstand
Sides

Roasted Sugar Snap Peas

Shirley Howie
Foxboro, MA

*This makes the perfect side dish to serve with any roasted
or grilled meats and can easily be doubled. They are
also good on their own as a tasty snack!*

1/2 lb. sugar snap peas,
   ends trimmed
1/2 c. red onion, sliced
1 T. olive oil

1 t. garlic powder
1 t. Italian seasoning
salt and pepper to taste

Combine all ingredients in a large bowl; toss to coat with oil. Spread
evenly on a lightly greased rimmed baking sheet. Bake at 425 degrees
for 10 to 12 minutes, until crisp-tender, stirring once while baking.
Makes 4 servings.

Oven-Fried Cauliflower

Julie Perkins
Anderson, IN

Easy and delicious!

1 c. mayonnaise
1 head cauliflower, cut
   into flowerets

1-1/2 c. Italian-flavored dry
   bread crumbs

Spoon mayonnaise into a plastic zipping bag; add cauliflower. Seal and
shake to coat. Add bread crumbs to a separate bag; add half of cauliflower
to bag. Seal bag and shake to coat; spread on a greased baking sheet.
Repeat with remaining cauliflower. Bake at 350 degrees for one hour,
or until tender. Serves 4.

Take the kids along when you visit a
farmstand. Let each child choose a
vegetable and let them help prepare it.
Even picky eaters may be won over!

Spring & Summer
Recipes for Sharing

Grilled Corn with Jalapeño Lime Butter

Carolyn Deckard
Bedford, IN

This recipe was given to me by a neighbor and it's my son-in-law Butch's favorite. The flavored butter is really tasty.

10 ears sweet corn, husks
　removed
2 T. olive oil

1 T. kosher salt
1 t. coarse pepper

Make Jalapeño Lime Butter ahead of time; chill. Rub ears of corn with olive oil; sprinkle evenly with salt and pepper. Place on grill over high heat; close grill lid. Cook, turning often, for 10 to 15 minutes or until tender. Serve with prepared butter. Serves 10.

Jalapeño Lime Butter:

3/4 c. butter, softened
2 jalapeño peppers, seeded
　and minced

2 T. lime zest
1 t. lime juice

Blend together all ingredients; shape into a 6-inch log. Wrap in wax paper or plastic wrap; chill for one hour.

Centerpieces that show off the red, white & blue couldn't be easier. Simply fill jelly jars with red, white & blue marbles, then tuck in mini pinwheels...so clever!

Farmstand
Sides

Cheesy Zucchini Patties

Shirl Parsons
Cape Carteret, NC

My mom used to make these crispy, cheesy zucchini patties with zucchini fresh-picked from our garden. Add more or less flour depending on how juicy the zucchini are.

2 to 3 large zucchini, shredded
3/4 c. sweet onion, finely
  chopped
2 eggs, lightly beaten
3/4 c. shredded mozzarella
  cheese

1/2 c. grated Parmesan cheese
1/2 to 3/4 c. all-purpose flour
salt and pepper to taste
2 T. oil
Garnish: sour cream or warm
  pasta sauce

Squeeze out excess moisture from zucchini; place in a large bowl. Add onion, eggs, cheeses and flour; mix well. Form mixture into patties by 1/4 cupfuls; season with salt and pepper. Heat oil in a large skillet over medium heat. Add patties and cook for 4 to 5 minutes, until golden; flip and cook other side. Serve topped with sour cream or warm pasta sauce. Serves 4 to 6.

Make some tangy pickled veggies next time you finish a jar of dill pickles! Simply cut up raw carrots, green peppers, celery and other vegetables, drop them into the leftover pickle juice and refrigerate.

Spring & Summer
Recipes for Sharing

Baked Cheesy Asparagus

Paula Marchesi
Auburn, PA

Fresh asparagus in a rich, creamy sauce goes perfectly with baked ham for Easter and other meals throughout spring and summer.

3 lbs. asparagus, trimmed
1 c. whipping cream
1/2 t. salt
1/2 t. pepper

1-1/2 c. shredded mozzarella
   cheese
1 c. grated Parmesan cheese
1 c. chopped pecans

Arrange asparagus in a greased 13"x9" baking pan. Drizzle with cream; season with salt and pepper. Top with cheeses and pecans. Bake, uncovered, at 400 degrees for 20 to 30 minutes, until asparagus is tender and cheese is melted and golden. Set pan on a wire rack; let stand for 5 minutes before serving. Serves 10.

Save flowers from special occasions and let them dry naturally. Tucked into a vase or turned into potpourri, they will be a sweet reminder of a wedding bouquet, a Mothers' Day corsage or a walk through Grandma's garden.

Farmstand
Sides

Yummy Lemon Orzo

Laurie Netolicky
Mount Prospect, IL

My kids love this super-easy orzo pasta! It's a great alternative to the usual side dishes. It's also refreshing and light for warm summer days.

2 T. butter
1 t. garlic, minced
2 c. orzo pasta, uncooked
4 c. chicken broth

1/2 to 1 lemon, halved
Optional: shredded Parmesan
    cheese

Melt butter in a large saucepan over low heat. Stir in garlic and sauté for one to 2 minutes. Add uncooked orzo; increase heat to medium. Cook for 3 to 4 minutes, stirring occasionally, until orzo starts to turn lightly golden. Stir in chicken broth. Cover and simmer for 15 to 20 minutes, until most of the liquid is absorbed. Squeeze in the juice of 1/2 lemon and stir. For a lot more lemon flavor, squeeze in another 1/2 lemon. Garnish with Parmesan cheese, if desired. Makes 6 servings.

Speedy Black Beans & Rice

Irene Robinson
Cincinnati, OH

This is a wonderful side dish to take on a picnic, or to serve with chicken or fish tacos on the grill.

8.8-oz. pkg. microwave
    ready-to-serve Spanish rice
15-1/2 oz. can black beans,
    drained and rinsed
4-oz. can chopped green chiles

2 T. fresh cilantro, chopped
Garnish: sour cream, salsa,
    diced tomatoes, shredded
    Cheddar cheese

Cook rice according to package directions; set aside. Combine beans and chiles in a microwave-safe dish; microwave for 1-1/2 minutes. Stir in hot rice and cilantro. Serve with toppings of your choice. Makes 3 to 4 servings.

Spring & Summer
Recipes for Sharing

Roasted Spring Asparagus

Kristy Wells
Ocala, FL

My family is absolutely crazy about fresh asparagus!
We know it's spring when it arrives in our local
grocery. Serve alongside your favorite meal.

2 to 3 lbs. fresh asparagus, trimmed
3 to 4 T. olive oil
Greek seasoning and salt to taste

In a large bowl, toss asparagus in olive oil to coat well. Arrange on a large baking sheet in a single layer; sprinkle with seasonings. Set pan on center rack of oven. Broil for 7 to 10 minutes, turning occasionally, until asparagus is toasty and golden. Serves 6 to 8.

Roasted Garlic Mushrooms

Jill Valentine
Jackson, TN

A delicious topper for steaks on the grill. Use white button
mushrooms or an assortment of different mushrooms.

1 lb. mushrooms, trimmed and halved
2 T. olive oil
1/8 t. salt
1/8 t. pepper
1 clove garlic, minced
1 T. fresh thyme, minced
1 T. balsamic vinegar

Arrange mushrooms on a baking sheet in a single layer. Drizzle with olive oil; season with salt and pepper. Bake at 450 degrees for 15 minutes; turn mushrooms and bake for 5 to 10 minutes more. Immediately transfer to a large bowl. Add garlic and thyme; toss to coat. Add vinegar and toss again. Makes 4 servings.

Save leftover odds & ends of cooked veggies...
they'll make tasty addition to soups.

Chilled &
Hot Soups
for Sharing

Spring & Summer
Recipes for Sharing

Shrimp Cocktail Soup

Paige Woodard
Loveland, CO

We enjoy this chilled soup as a special treat every 4th of July! It's become a bit of a tradition for our family to begin our picnic with this cold soup. Perfect for a fancy summer patio party, too. It's easy to adjust the ingredients to what everyone likes best...more cucumber, less tomato and so forth. Garnish with a few shrimp skewered on long toothpicks, just for fun.

1 lb. cooked salad shrimp or
    extra-small shrimp, peeled
    and tails cut off
1 lb. crabmeat or imitation
    crabmeat, flaked or chopped
2 avocados, peeled, pitted
    and diced
2 cucumbers, diced

2 roma tomatoes, diced
3 to 4 green onions, chopped
1 jalapeño pepper, finely diced
1/4 to 1/2 c. fresh cilantro,
    chopped
2 T. lime juice
64-oz. bottle plain or clam-
    flavored tomato juice, to taste

In a large bowl, mix together all ingredients except tomato juice; mix well. Add tomato juice to desired consistency. Cover and refrigerate for 2 hours to overnight to allow flavors to blend. Serve chilled in cups, garnished with small shrimp picks. Makes 10 to 12 servings.

Bruschetta is an easy, delicious snack that's perfect alongside chilled summer soups. Combine 2 diced ripe tomatoes, a teaspoon of olive oil and 1/2 teaspoon chopped fresh basil. Spread over toasted slices of Italian bread.

Chilled & Hot Soups
for Sharing

Veggie Potato-Leek Soup

Lynne Thompson
Asbury, NJ

I love potato-leek soup. Always liked to stir it up for the kids, to get more veggies into them. I started to add more veggies and half-blend it...they really like it that way! Use half-and-half for a richer flavor.

2 leeks, white portion
   only, chopped
3 T. butter
4 to 5 Yukon Gold potatoes,
   peeled and cut into
   1-inch cubes

1 carrot, peeled and chopped
3 to 4 c. chicken broth
1 to 1-1/2 c. fresh spinach, torn
1/4 c. half-and-half or milk
salt and pepper to taste

In a large saucepan over medium heat, cook leeks in butter until lightly golden. Add potatoes, carrot and enough chicken broth to cover vegetables. Simmer for 25 minutes, or until potatoes are soft. Add spinach; cook and stir until wilted. Stir in half-and-half or milk. Using a potato masher, mash until potatoes and veggies are half-mashed, or more if you like a smoother soup. Or, use an immersion blender to blend to desired consistency. Season with salt and pepper. Serve warm or at room temperature. Makes 6 servings.

Creating an herb wreath is easy! Bundle together fresh herbs like bay leaves, basil, oregano, sage and marjoram. Wire onto a straw wreath. Hanging in the kitchen, it's easy to snip herbs for any recipe.

Spring & Summer
Recipes for Sharing

Crowd-Pleasing Chili

Nancy Kailihiwa
Wheatland, CA

I work with a group of high school students as an academic tech. To encourage them to work hard, I promised to make them my semi-famous crowd-pleasing chili. Not only did they work hard, they went over and above! So I made chocolate chip cookies for them too. I'm always asked for this when we do the high school's football team fundraiser...it sells out each time.

2 lbs. lean ground beef
1 c. yellow onion, diced
2 28-oz. cans diced tomatoes
2 28-oz. cans crushed tomatoes
28-oz. can tomato sauce
2 15-1/2 oz. cans chili beans
2 15-1/2 oz. cans red kidney
   beans, drained and rinsed

1 T. garlic, minced
1/4 c. chili powder
2 T. ground cumin
1 c. shredded sharp Cheddar
   cheese
Garnish: additional shredded
   cheese, chopped onions,
   sour cream

Brown beef in a large skillet over medium heat; drain. Add onion; sauté until semi-translucent. Transfer beef mixture to an 8-quart slow cooker. Stir in diced and crushed tomatoes with juice, tomato sauce, all beans, garlic and seasonings; top with shredded cheese. Cover and cook on low setting for 4 to 6 hours. (May also use an 18-quart roaster oven; cook at 300 degrees for 2 hours and turn to low to keep warm.) At serving time, stir again; garnish with desired toppings. Makes 20 to 30 servings.

Serve up Crowd-Pleasing Chili chuck wagon style. Spoon chili into enamelware bowls, add a side of cornbread and keep bandannas on hand for terrific lap-size napkins.

Chilled & Hot Soups
for Sharing

Brunswick Stew

Jason Keller
Carrollton, GA

We love this hearty old-fashioned stew...it's perfect for cooking up over a campfire. Serve with crusty bread or cornbread.

1 T. olive oil
16-oz. pkg. frozen chopped
 onions & peppers, thawed
16-oz. pkg. pulled smoked pork
 or chicken in sauce
1/2 c. barbecue sauce
28-oz. can diced tomatoes

8-oz. pkg. frozen corn, thawed
8-oz. pkg. frozen baby lima
 beans, thawed
salt and pepper to taste
Optional: chopped fresh parsley,
 hot pepper sauce

Heat oil in a Dutch oven over medium-high heat. Add onions and peppers; sauté for 6 to 8 minutes. Stir in pork or chicken and barbecue sauce; cook and stir for one minute. Add tomatoes with juice, corn and beans; season with salt and pepper. Bring to a boil over high heat. Reduce to medium-low; simmer for 15 minutes, stirring occasionally. If desired, garnish with parsley; serve with hot sauce on the side. Makes 8 servings.

Asiago Bread Sticks

Cindy Neel
Gooseberry Patch

Perfect for dipping into saucy soups.

1 egg, beaten
1 T. water
1 t. Dijon mustard
3/4 c. shredded Asiago cheese

4-1/2 t. sesame seed
1/2 t. garlic powder
11-oz. tube refrigerated bread
 sticks, separated

Whisk together egg, water and mustard in a shallow dish. In another shallow dish, combine cheese, sesame seed and garlic powder. Dip each bread stick into egg mixture; coat with cheese mixture. Twist bread sticks several times; place one inch apart on a sprayed baking sheet. Firmly press down ends. Bake at 350 degrees for 14 to 19 minutes, until golden. Serve warm. Makes one dozen.

Spring & Summer
Recipes for Sharing

Chunky Corn & Tomato Gazpacho

Vickie
Gooseberry Patch

This chilled soup is so refreshing after a day in the sunshine...use your fresh veggie finds from the farmers' market! Top soup bowls with a dollop of sour cream or yogurt and a sprig of fresh basil.

1 c. corn kernels
2 yellow tomatoes, chopped
3 c. tomato juice
1 cucumber, diced
1/2 c. onion, minced
1 clove garlic, minced

3 T. lime juice
2 T. fresh basil, chopped
1/2 t. salt
1/4 t. pepper
1/4 t. chili powder

In a large bowl, combine all ingredients; mix well. Cover and chill for one hour before serving. Serves 6.

One of my best memories of my daddy is going to the Great Smoky Mountains on vacation. My daddy, mom, niece and I would load the car with all the essentials and off we'd go. Daddy would always have to blow the horn while passing through East River and Big Walker Tunnels on our way to the mountains. For our lunch, Mom would pack all the necessities for sandwiches and snacks, and Daddy would always stop by a local farmers' stand and buy fresh tomatoes for our sandwiches. We always had to have a bucket of chicken, too, and biscuits. Every summer, I have to have a fresh tomato sandwich and it takes me back a lifetime ago. My daddy has been gone for more than 30 years, but not a day goes by that I don't think of him and those family vacations and tomato sandwiches.

–Amy Thomason Hunt, Traphill, NC

Chilled & Hot Soups
for Sharing

Sweet Cornbread

Hollie Moots
Marysville, OH

This cornbread is perfect to accompany your favorite soup or chili. Leftovers even make a yummy breakfast treat, slathered with butter and jam!

1-1/2 c. all-purpose flour	1/3 c. oil
1/2 c. cornmeal	3 T. butter, melted
2/3 c. sugar	1 T. honey
1 T. baking powder	2 eggs, beaten
1/2 t. salt	1-1/4 c. milk

In a large bowl, combine flour, cornmeal, sugar, baking powder and salt; mix well. Add remaining ingredients; mix well. Pour batter into a greased 13"x9" baking pan. Bake at 350 degrees for 30 to 35 minutes, until set in the center and lightly golden. Cut into squares. Makes 12 servings.

Decorate small note pads with clippings from seed packet. Useful for making shopping lists for the next trip to the farmers' market...sweet favors at a garden party, too!

Spring & Summer
Recipes for Sharing

Picked-from-the-Garden Soup

Sandy Coffey
Cincinnati, OH

This is a sure-fire farmers' market kind of soup. It's meatless yet tasty. Other fresh veggies can be added as desired, such as carrots, cauliflower and mushrooms. It freezes really well, too...a great way to enjoy fresh vegetables later.

1 head cabbage, chopped
1 bunch celery, chopped
3 onions, chopped
2 green peppers, chopped

4 ripe tomatoes, chopped
6 to 8 cubes chicken bouillon
salt and pepper to taste

Combine all vegetables in a large soup kettle. Add enough water to cover vegetables; add bouillon, salt and pepper. Bring to a boil over medium-high heat. Reduce heat to medium-low. Simmer until vegetables are tender, adding more water as needed to desired consistency. Makes 10 to 12 servings.

Chive Biscuits

Constance Lewis
Florence, AL

So easy...no need for a biscuit cutter!

2 c. self-rising flour
1 T. baking powder
1 t. salt
6 T. shortening

2 T. fresh chives, chopped
2/3 to 1 c. buttermilk
Optional: melted butter

In a bowl, combine flour, baking powder and salt. Add shortening; mix with 2 forks until mixture resembles small peas. Add chives and 2/3 cup buttermilk; stir just until combined. If mixture is too dry to form into a ball, stir in more buttermilk. Place dough on a floured surface; work gently with hands into a 10-inch by 6-inch rectangle. Transfer to a lightly greased baking sheet. With a sharp knife, score dough into 8 pieces, but do not cut apart. Bake at 450 degrees for 14 minutes, or until deeply golden. Brush tops with butter, if desired. Makes 8 biscuits.

Chilled & Hot Soups
for Sharing

Cream of Homegrown Tomato Soup *Pat Martin*
Riverside, CA

I put together this recipe one year when family & friends gifted me with their bountiful tomato garden results. I have served this hot or cold and like to spice it up depending on my mood. For a little heat, add a bit of cayenne pepper, hot sauce or Mexican chili-lime salt. This is great served hot, or sipped cold from a canning jar!

10 to 12 ripe tomatoes
1 t. baking soda
1/4 c. butter
1 onion, diced
1/4 c. all-purpose flour

2 t. garlic, minced
1 to 2 t. salt
1/2 t. pepper
6 c. whole milk
2 to 3 t. fresh basil, chopped

Add whole tomatoes to a large saucepan of boiling water. Boil for several minutes; drain. Cool tomatoes slightly; peel and chop coarsely. Measure 6 cups tomatoes and set aside. In a bowl, combine tomatoes and baking soda; mix well and set aside. In a large stockpot, melt butter over medium heat. Sauté onion for 3 to 4 minutes, until translucent. Add flour to onion mixture. Cook and stir for one to 2 minutes, just until very lightly golden. Add tomatoes, garlic, salt and pepper; simmer over medium heat for 5 to 6 minutes. Stir in milk and basil; cook over low heat for 5 minutes, or until heated through. Using an immersion blender, process mixture until smooth. (May also add small batches to a blender; process carefully and return to stockpot.) Season with more salt and pepper, if needed. Serves 6 to 8.

Try something new with tomato soup...grilled cheese croutons! Make grilled cheese sandwiches as usual, then slice them into small squares. Toss into bowls of soup and serve.

Spring & Summer
Recipes for Sharing

Triple Corn Chowder

Victoria Mitchel
Gettysburg, PA

I came up with this recipe on a whim, to use up some sweet corn that was left over from dinner the previous night. I grabbed my pen and started writing down what I was doing, and I'm so glad I did! My daughter and husband loved this soup and have asked me to make it again several times. You could use frozen corn, I'm sure, but fresh or leftover sweet corn just adds a little something "extra."

2 T. olive oil
5 ears sweet corn, kernels cut off
5 green onions, sliced
3 stalks celery, sliced
4 c. chicken broth
15-1/4 oz. can corn, drained
14-3/4 oz. can creamed corn
1 bay leaf

1/2 t. smoked paprika
1/2 t. dried thyme
1 t. salt
1 t. pepper
1 c. whipping cream
Garnish: shredded Parmesan
   cheese, additional thyme

Heat oil in a skillet over medium heat. Sauté corn until beginning to turn golden. Add onions and celery; sauté until softened. Add chicken broth and both cans of corn; return to a boil. Reduce heat to medium-low; stir in seasonings. Cover and simmer over low heat for about 45 minutes, stirring occasionally. Discard bay leaf. Stir in cream and serve with Parmesan cheese and thyme. Makes 4 to 6 servings.

Summer afternoon...summer afternoon;
to me those have always been the two most
beautiful words in the English language.
–Henry James

Chilled & Hot Soups
for Sharing

Marta's Nacho Cheese Soup

Marta Norton
Redlands, CA

Homemade salsa puts this recipe over the top...
but your favorite salsa will work as well.

1/2 c. butter
1/2 c. all-purpose flour
3 c. whole milk
16-oz. pkg. shredded
    Cheddar cheese
2 14-oz. cans chicken broth

1/2 t. salt
1/4 t. pepper
1-1/2 c. Rebecca's Famous Salsa
    (see p. 158), or other salsa
Optional: tortilla chips
Garnish: jalapeño pepper slices

Melt butter in a large saucepan over medium heat. Add flour and cook for one minute, stirring until smooth and lightly golden. Whisk in milk. Add cheese; cook and stir until completely melted and blended. Stir in chicken broth, salt and pepper. Continue cooking until soup begins to bubble. Reduce heat to low; stir in salsa. Continue cooking until soup is thick and creamy. If desired, add tortilla chips to soup at serving time to add crunch. Garnish with jalapeño slices. Serves 8 to 10.

A chopped salad of lettuce, tomatoes and radishes goes well alongside a south-of-the-border soup. Drizzle with a tasty lime dressing. To make, whisk together 1/3 cup olive oil and 1/3 cup lime juice. Season with hot pepper sauce, salt and pepper to taste.

Spring & Summer
Recipes for Sharing

Chilled Cherry & Lemon Mint Soup

Paula Marchesi
Auburn, PA

This soup is delicious quick & easy to make with fresh cherries, my favorite...frozen cherries will work well too.

3/4 lb. sweet cherries, pitted
   and divided
1/4 c. sugar
1 T. lemon mint leaves,
   loosely packed

1/2 t. vanilla extract
1 c. vanilla yogurt
Optional: lemon juice to taste
Garnish: additional vanilla
   yogurt

Halve one cup cherries; set aside. In a blender, combine remaining cherries, sugar, mint leaves and vanilla. Process until smooth. Add yogurt; pulse just until blended in. Add lemon juice to taste, if desired for more flavor. Stir in reserved cherries. Cover and chill. At serving time, ladle soup into small bowls or cups; drizzle with additional yogurt. Makes 2 to 3 servings.

Easter Soup

Julie Perkins
Anderson, IN

This refreshing chilled soup is just right for a spring luncheon.

1 lb. carrots, peeled and shredded
1 c. orange juice
1 c. apricot nectar
1/2 c. water

1/3 c. honey
1/3 c. sour cream
1/4 c. lemon juice

Combine carrots, orange juice, apricot nectar and water in a large saucepan. Cook over high heat until almost boiling. Reduce heat to medium-low. Simmer for 20 minutes, stirring occasionally. Stir in remaining ingredients.
Serve chilled or at room temperature.
Makes 2 to 3 servings.

Chilled & Hot Soups
for Sharing

Cold Strawberry Soup

Marcia Marcoux
Charlton, MA

Ideal for a spring ladies' luncheon.

1 pt. strawberries, hulled,
   sliced and divided
1 c. sour cream
1/2 c. whole milk

1/2 c. ginger ale
6 T. sugar, or to taste
1 t. vanilla extract
1 T. lemon juice

Set aside 3 to 4 sliced strawberries for garnish. In a blender, combine remaining strawberries and other ingredients; process until smooth. Transfer to a covered container; chill. Serve in frosted bowls or cups, garnished with reserved strawberries. Serves 4.

Easy 2-Ingredient Biscuits

Suzi Bryant
Gray, GA

I was never able to make good homemade biscuits until
I found this recipe. Hope you like them too!

1 c. self-rising flour

1/2 to 3/4 c. whipping cream

Place flour in a bowl. Stir in cream a little at a time, until mixed. On a floured surface, knead dough 2 to 3 times. Roll out dough 1/2-inch thick and cut with a biscuit cutter, or pinch off bits and hand-roll. Place in a greased 9"x9" baking pan. Bake at 350 degrees for 15 to 20 minutes, until golden. Makes 6 biscuits.

For a sweet summertime glow, fill glass votive candleholders
with coarse salt, then tuck in a votive. The salt crystals
will sparkle in the flickering light.

Spring & Summer
Recipes for Sharing

Chilled Cucumber & Lime Soup

Vickie
Gooseberry Patch

*A refreshing cold soup for a sunny summer day. Make it
a day ahead to allow the flavors to blend.*

2 cucumbers, peeled, seeded
   and coarsely grated
1 c. half-and-half
1 c. plain yogurt
1 c. sour cream
2 T. lime zest
2 T. lime juice

2 T. fresh chives, snipped
1 T. shallots, finely chopped
salt and white pepper to taste
Optional: additional thinly sliced
   cucumber, snipped fresh
   chives, lime zest

In a large bowl, combine cucumber, half-and-half, yogurt, sour cream
and lime zest; stir well. Stir in lime juice, chives, shallots and seasonings.
Cover and chill overnight for the best flavor. To serve, ladle into chilled
bowls. Garnish with cucumber, snipped chives and a small amount of
lime zest, if you wish. Makes 6 to 8 servings.

Serving chilled soups at a picnic or party? Ladle them into
mini canning jars, add lids and place in an ice chest.
They'll be easy to set out on the party table and
everyone can easily help themselves.

Blackberry Cornbread Muffins

Tamela James
Grove City, OH

We have a local farm market that has the best blackberries. This recipe is a must when the blackberries are in season! I like to freeze the berries before adding, as they won't break apart.

2 c. self-rising white cornmeal
1/2 c. sugar
5 eggs, beaten
16-oz. container sour cream

1/2 c. butter, melted
2 c. frozen blackberries
Garnish: butter

In a large bowl, stir together cornmeal and sugar; make a well in the center and set aside. In another bowl, stir together eggs, sour cream and butter. Add egg mixture to well in cornmeal mixture; stir just until mixed. Gently fold in frozen blackberries. Spoon batter into greased muffin pans, filling 3/4 full. Bake at 450 degrees for 15 to 17 minutes, until tops are golden. Cool in pan for 5 minutes; serve warm with butter. Makes 2 dozen.

Store fresh summer berries to enjoy later. Simply place berries in a single layer on a baking sheet and freeze, then store in plastic freezer bags. Frozen this way, it's convenient to remove just the amount of berries you need for a recipe.

Spring & Summer
Recipes for Sharing

Prize Garden Chowder

Carol Kise
South Waterford, ME

Our family loves this chowder...all 3 generations of us. Back in 2000, I entered this recipe in a local newspaper's annual cooking contest. I won both First Place and Grand Prize! The following year, I won Grand Prize for another soup recipe, too.

1/2 c. green pepper, diced	3 cubes chicken bouillon
1/2 c. onion, diced	1 t. salt
1/4 c. butter	1/4 t. pepper
1 c. potatoes, peeled and diced	1/2 c. all-purpose flour
1 c. carrots, peeled and diced	2 c. milk
1 c. cauliflower, diced	1 T. fresh parsley, minced
1 c. broccoli, diced	1-1/2 c. shredded white
3 c. water	Cheddar cheese

In a Dutch oven over medium heat, sauté green pepper and onion in butter until tender. Add remaining vegetables, water, bouillon cubes, salt and pepper; bring to a boil. Reduce heat to medium-low. Cover and simmer for 20 minutes, or until vegetables are tender. In a cup, stir together flour and milk until smooth; stir into soup. Bring to a boil; cook and stir for 2 minutes. Stir in parsley. Just before serving, stir in cheese over low heat until melted. Makes 6 to 8 servings.

Cheese toast is delicious alongside savory soups, and a snap to make on a countertop grill. Spread softened butter over slices of Italian or sourdough bread, grill until golden, then sprinkle with fresh Parmesan cheese.

Chilled & Hot Soups
for Sharing

Grandma's Favorite Zucchini Bread
Julie Monk
Hillsboro, IL

I've been baking this bread for more than ten years now, after getting a huge zucchini harvest from my very first garden and not knowing what to do with all of them. I love whipping up a batch and giving it away as gifts. My husband even shares mini loaves with the guys at work. I like to use disposable foil pans for the mini loaves, then I can freeze them and pull out later for gifts, barter and trading...last-minute potlucks and cookouts with friends, too!

2 c. zucchini, shredded	2 t. vanilla extract
3 eggs, beaten	1 t. baking powder
1-1/2 c. sugar	1 t. baking soda
1/2 c. light brown sugar, packed	1 t. salt
1/2 c. unsweetened applesauce	1 T. cinnamon
1/2 c. oil	3 c. all-purpose flour

Place shredded zucchini in a bowl and set aside; do not drain any liquid that it may produce. In a separate large bowl, mix together eggs, sugars, applesauce, oil and vanilla; fold in zucchini. Mix in baking powder, baking soda, salt and cinnamon; stir in flour. Divide batter into 2 greased 9"x5" loaf pans or 4 greased 6"x3-1/2" disposable mini foil loaf pans. Bake at 325 degrees for 40 to 50 minutes, turning pans after 30 minutes, until a toothpick tests clean. (Start checking mini pans at 30 minutes.) Cool in pans for 5 minutes; turn out of pans and finish cooling on a wire rack. Serve right away, or wrap loaves in foil and freeze until needed. Makes 2 regular loaves or 4 mini loaves.

Fresh-baked, cooled bread freezes beautifully. Wrap it in plastic, then aluminum foil and freeze up to 3 weeks. Add a ribbon bow for a delightful hostess gift.

Spring & Summer
Recipes for Sharing

Springtime Soup

Sandra Erdman
Winona, MN

It was one of those "soup-feeling" days. Winter was trying to end; spring was having a hard time arriving. The house was on the cool side, but the sun was shining brightly outside. This soup day, I was set on using up as many vegetables from the refrigerator as possible. So this is what I came up with, and it was just right. I like making soup... you can be very creative with it and it usually ends up tasting good!

3 T. butter
3 leeks, white and green
    parts, chopped
1/2 c. onion, chopped
9 c. hot water
3 potatoes, peeled and
    thinly sliced

3 carrots, peeled and thinly sliced
2 to 3 t. salt
1/3 c. instant rice, uncooked
1 bunch asparagus, cut into
    1/2-inch pieces
1/2 lb. fresh spinach, chopped
1 c. light cream

Melt butter in a large soup pan over medium heat; add leeks and onion. Reduce heat to low and cook until tender, about 5 minutes. Add hot water, potatoes, carrots and salt; bring to a boil over high heat. Reduce heat to medium-low; simmer for 15 minutes. Add rice and asparagus; simmer for 25 minutes. Add spinach and simmer for 10 minutes. Stir in cream; bring just to a boil, but do not boil. For best flavor, cover and chill overnight before serving; heat through at serving time. Serves 8 to 10.

At summer yard sales, watch for big, old-fashioned enamelware stockpots. They're just right for cooking up lots of soup for sharing.

Chilled & Hot Soups
for Sharing

New England Summer Squash Soup

Evelyn North
Leominster, ME

I had this soup at a steakhouse at a summer birthday lunch and loved it. So I asked the chef, and he gave me his recipe. So tasty and light for hot days.

2 T. butter
1 onion, chopped
3 small yellow squash,
  seeded and chopped

1 to 2 c. chicken broth
12-oz. can evaporated milk
garlic powder, salt and/or pepper
  to taste

Melt butter in a saucepan over medium heat. Add onion; cook until golden. Add squash; cook until crisp-tender. Add desired amount of chicken broth; simmer until squash is tender. Purée in a blender or mash squash in pan. Stir in remaining ingredients; heat through, but do not boil. Serves 4.

Cream of Asparagus Soup

Elaine Slabinski
Monroe Twp., NJ

My husband grows asparagus which is very plentiful in the spring. This is a quick, easy, and delicious recipe.

1 bunch fresh asparagus,
  trimmed and sliced
2 T. onion, thinly sliced

1-1/2 c. chicken broth
1/2 c. half-and-half
salt and pepper to taste

In a saucepan over medium heat, combine asparagus, onion and chicken broth. Cook until tender. Purée in a blender; return to saucepan. Stir in half-and-half; heat through, but do not boil. Add seasonings and serve. Makes 4 servings.

Herbed crackers make any soup even tastier! Toss together 1-1/2 cups oyster crackers, 1-1/2 tablespoons melted butter, 1/4 teaspoon dried thyme and 1/4 teaspoon garlic powder. Spread on a baking sheet and bake at 350 degrees for about 10 minutes.

Spring & Summer
Recipes for Sharing

Summer Veggie Soup

Debby Marcum
New Castle, IN

My husband's Aunt Tootie gave me this meatless soup recipe years ago. It is one of our favorites. I love to bring in the fresh veggies from the garden and put on a pot of this soup for dinner. If you don't have fresh ingredients available, canned will work fine. Tastes even better the next day!

2/3 c. carrots, peeled and sliced
1/2 c. onion, diced
2 cloves garlic, chopped
3 c. chicken broth
1-1/2 c. cabbage, chopped
1/2 c. green beans, trimmed

1 T. tomato paste
1/2 t. chopped basil
1/4 t. dried oregano
1/4 t. salt
1/2 c. zucchini, sliced

Spray a large saucepan with non-stick vegetable spray. Add carrots, onion and garlic; cook over medium heat until onion is golden. Add chicken broth, cabbage, beans, tomato paste and seasonings. Reduce heat to medium-low. Simmer for 45 minutes to one hour, until vegetables are nearly tender. Add zucchini and cook until tender. Makes 6 to 8 servings.

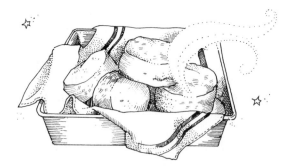

Try this honey-berry spread...scrumptious on warm biscuits.
In a blender, combine one pint stemmed strawberries,
one tablespoon lemon juice and 1/2 cup honey. Process until
smooth. Pour into a saucepan and simmer over low heat
20 minutes; stirring occasionally. Makes 1-1/2 cups.

Chilled & Hot Soups
for Sharing

Mimi's Banana Bread

Joan Raven
Cicero, NY

My heart fills with pure joy when my grandsons ask me, "Mimi, can you please bake one banana bread just for me and one for my brother? It's the best banana bread ever!"

1/2 c. butter, softened
1 c. sugar
2 eggs, lightly beaten
1 c. ripe bananas, mashed
1-1/2 T. buttermilk
1 t. lemon juice

2 c. all-purpose flour
1-1/2 t. baking powder
1/2 t. baking soda
1/4 t. salt
1/2 c. chopped walnuts or pecans

In a large bowl, blend butter and sugar; stir in eggs and set aside. In another bowl, combine bananas, buttermilk and lemon juice; mix well and add to butter mixture. Add flour, baking powder, baking soda and salt; mix well. Gently fold in nuts. Pour batter into a greased 9"x5" loaf pan. Bake at 350 degrees for 45 to 50 minutes. Makes one loaf.

On family trips, let everyone pick out their own picture postcards. Have them sign and date the cards, then add their comments about each site. Back home, punch 2 holes on the side and tie with ribbon to make a little book. A fun little memento!

Spring & Summer
Recipes for Sharing

Lemon-Blueberry Biscuits

Becky Kuchenbecker
Ravenna, OH

After I tasted these delicious biscuits at a family gathering, I just had to have the recipe. I love the combination of lemon and blueberries.

2 c. all-purpose flour
1/3 c. sugar
2 t. baking powder
1/2 t. baking soda
1/4 t. salt

8-oz. container lemon yogurt
1 egg, lightly beaten
1/4 c. butter, melted
1 t. lemon zest
1 c. blueberries

In a large bowl, combine flour, sugar, baking powder, baking soda and salt; mix well and set aside. In another bowl, stir together yogurt, egg, butter and lemon zest. Add to flour mixture; stir just until moistened. Fold in blueberries. Drop batter by heaping tablespoonfuls onto a greased baking sheet. Bake at 400 degrees for 15 to 18 minutes, until lightly golden. Drizzle Glaze over warm biscuits. Makes about one dozen.

Glaze:

1/2 c. powdered sugar
1 T. lemon juice

1/2 t. lemon zest

Combine all ingredients; mix to a glaze consistency.

Just living is not enough. One must have sunshine, freedom and a little flower.
–Hans Christian Anderson

Chilled & Hot Soups
for Sharing

White Gazpacho

Arlene Smulski
Lyons, IL

Looking for a gazpacho that isn't made with tomatoes? This is the one for you...it's creamy and tangy. Add a pinch of white pepper to add another depth of flavor.

1-1/4 lbs. English cucumbers, peeled and chopped
1 c. seedless green grapes
1 slice country-style Italian bread, cubed and crusts removed
1/2 c. slivered almonds
1/4 c. shallot, finely chopped
1/2 t. kosher salt
1 c. plain Greek yogurt
1 T. sherry vinegar or red wine vinegar
Garnish: fresh mint leaves, cucumber slices

In a large bowl, combine cucumbers, grapes, bread cubes, almonds, shallot and salt. Cover and chill for 2 hours. With an immersion blender, process mixture until nearly smooth. Press through a fine-mesh sieve into a bowl; discard solids. Whisk in yogurt and vinegar. Serve immediately, or cover and chill up to 24 hours. At serving time, garnish with mint and cucumber. Makes 4 servings.

White-washed clay pots planted with fragrant herbs make classic cookout table centerpieces.

Spring & Summer
Recipes for Sharing

Summer Chicken & Vegetable Soup

JoAnn
Gooseberry Patch

We love our chicken soup year 'round. Sometimes I add a handful of mini farfalle pasta along with the carrots...my kids used to say the noodles look like tiny butterflies!

1 onion, chopped
1 T. olive oil
1 t. garlic, minced
2 ripe tomatoes, diced
1 t. fresh thyme, chopped
4 c. vegetable broth
1 bay leaf
3 boneless, skinless
    chicken breasts

1 c. carrots, peeled and diced
1 green pepper, diced
1 yellow squash, diced
1 T. lemon zest
1/4 t. salt
1/4 t. pepper

In a soup pot, sauté onion in olive oil for 3 to 4 minutes, until translucent. Add garlic; cook for 30 seconds. Stir in tomatoes and thyme; cook for 4 minutes. Add vegetable broth and bay leaf; bring to a boil. Add chicken; return to a simmer. Reduce heat to medium-low. Simmer for 8 to 10 minutes, just until chicken is cooked through. Remove chicken to a plate; set aside to cool. Add carrots and green pepper to broth; cook for 5 minutes, or until carrots are tender. Add squash, lemon zest and seasonings; simmer another 4 minutes. Just before serving, discard bay leaf. Shred chicken; stir into soup and serve. Serves 8.

When driving in the country, if you see a sign for a tag or barn sale, don't pass it by! You're sure to find oodles of ideas for bringing whimsy to your kitchen and garden back home.

Chilled & Hot Soups
for Sharing

Chilled Fire-Roasted Tomato Soup

Wendy Meadows
Spring Hill, FL

My grandma used to love tomato soup, but felt it was too hot in the summer to enjoy it. So I played with ingredients until I found a chilled tomato soup she liked. It also allowed me to use up the cases of fire-roasted tomatoes my son brought home! My grandmother is no longer here with me, but this recipe brings back memories of Monday lunches with her.

14-1/2 oz. can fire-roasted
    diced tomatoes
1-1/2 c. tomato juice
1 c. cucumber, peeled and diced

1/4 c. red pepper, diced
2 T. red onion, diced
2 T. fresh cilantro, snipped
2 t. white wine vinegar

Combine undrained tomatoes and remaining ingredients in a food processor. Process with quick on-and-off motions until mixture is coarsely puréed. Cover and refrigerate at least one hour; best if allowed to chill overnight. Makes 4 servings.

Chicken Lemon-Rice Soup

Lisa Rischar
Cedar Lake, IN

Sometimes you just need a bowl of chicken soup...even in the summertime! Although I'm not Greek, this soup is. I enjoy it at a local Greek diner, but it is easy to replicate at home.

4 c. chicken broth
1/2 c. instant rice, uncooked
2 eggs, beaten

juice of 2 lemons
2 c. cooked chicken breast,
    shredded

In a stockpot over medium-high heat, bring chicken broth to a boil. Add rice; reduce heat to low. Simmer for about 20 minutes; remove from heat. Whisk together eggs and lemon juice in a bowl. Slowly add egg mixture to the warm broth, one tablespoon at a time, whisking constantly so the egg does not cook. Add chicken; stir to warm through and serve. Makes 4 servings.

Spring & Summer
Recipes for Sharing

End-of-Summer Chicken Tortilla Soup

Victoria Mitchel
Gettysburg, PA

I came up with this recipe one day when I had all kinds of leftovers in my refrigerator. In case it turned out well, I jotted down all the ingredients with their measurements as I went along. I'm so glad I did...my son and I loved it! We managed to save some so that my husband could enjoy it as well. It's a great soup to use up all those summer leftovers and it's healthy, which is always a plus!

1 T. olive oil
1/2 onion, chopped
2 cloves garlic, minced
32-oz. container chicken broth
3 cubes chicken bouillon
1-1/2 c. cooked chicken,
    shredded or cubed
2 14-1/2 oz. cans black beans,
    drained and rinsed
3 ears corn, kernels cut off,
    or 1-1/2 c. frozen corn

4 c. favorite salsa
1 c. water
2 T. tomato paste
1 t. chili powder
1/2 t. dried cumin
1/4 t. dried oregano
1/2 t. salt
juice of one lime
Garnish: shredded Mexican-
    blend cheese, tortilla chips,
    sour cream

Heat oil in a large soup pan over medium heat. Add onion; cook until translucent. Add garlic; cook and stir about one minute, until fragrant. Add chicken broth and bouillon cubes. Simmer for about 10 minutes. Add chicken, beans and corn; stir well. Add remaining ingredients except garnish. Simmer over low heat for about one hour to allow flavors to blend together. Ladle into bowls; garnish with desired toppings and serve. Serves 8 to 10.

Save those extra herbs from the garden! Spoon chopped fresh herbs into an ice cube tray, one tablespoon per cube. Cover with water and freeze. Frozen cubes can be dropped right into a pot of hot soup.

Backyard
Cookouts
& Easy Suppers

Spring & Summer
Recipes for Sharing

Gram J's Chicken Marinade

Shirley Jackson
Hazel, KY

Every summer, the firemen from our little hometown of Chaffee, New York would host chicken barbecues. My mother-in-law was in charge of the barbecue sauce. Over the years of making this, I found that using the sauce as a marinade also tenderized the chicken! Serve the chicken warm, or chill and use in chicken salads.

1 pasteurized egg	1 T. salt
1/2 c. corn or canola oil	1/4 t. pepper
1 c. cider vinegar	4 pieces chicken
1-1/2 t. poultry seasoning	

Beat egg in a large bowl. Add remaining ingredients except chicken; mix until well blended. Add chicken, making sure marinade covers chicken. Cover and refrigerate for 4 to 6 hours. Drain, discarding marinade. Grill chicken over medium heat, turning frequently, until a meat thermometer inserted in the thickest piece reads 165 degrees. Turn grill to high; continue to cook until skin is crisp. Makes 4 servings.

Invite friends and neighbors to a good old-fashioned block party. Set up picnic tables, arrange lots of chairs in the shade and encourage everyone to bring a favorite dish. You'll make some wonderful memories together!

118

Backyard Cookouts
& Easy Suppers

Spinach Lemon Rigatoni
Lisa Ann Panzino DiNunzio
Vineland, NJ

Perfect springtime pasta...light, yet oh-so flavorful! The pasta can also be topped with grilled chicken breasts, toasted pine nuts or walnuts, or marinated mushrooms. Make this dish your own!

16-oz. pkg. rigatoni pasta,
  uncooked
3 c. baby spinach
1/4 c. extra-virgin olive oil
2 T. butter

2 t. lemon zest
2 T. lemon juice
sea salt and pepper to taste
Optional: grated Parmesan
  cheese

Cook pasta according to directions on package; drain. Return pasta to pasta pot and set off stove. Add spinach, olive oil, butter, lemon zest and lemon juice to warm pasta. Gently toss together until spinach slightly wilts. Season with salt and pepper; toss again. Sprinkle servings with Parmesan cheese, if desired. Makes 4 to 6 servings.

Pick up a dozen pint-size Mason jars...they're fun
and practical for serving ice-cold lemonade,
sweet tea or frosty root beer!

Spring & Summer
Recipes for Sharing

Pork Tenderloin with Apricot Glaze

Nancy Labedz
Channahon, IL

This is a special meal we had on Easter, served with mashed potatoes, fresh asparagus and hot rolls. Sometimes we had baked ham instead, and this glaze was good on the ham as well.

2-lb. pork tenderloin
12-oz. jar apricot preserves
1/3 c. lemon juice
1/3 c. catsup

1/4 c. chicken broth
3 T. honey
1 T. soy sauce
1/8 t. ground ginger

Place pork tenderloin in a lightly greased shallow 13"x9" baking pan. Bake, uncovered, at 350 degrees for 30 to 35 minutes. Combine remaining ingredients in a saucepan over medium heat. Cook and stir until heated through. Slice pork; drizzle with glaze. Serve remaining glaze in a gravy boat alongside sliced pork. Serves 6.

Teriyaki Pork Ribs

Karen Ensign
Providence, UT

Our whole family loves this flavorful grilled pork! The marinade works well with thick-cut pork chops too.

2 lbs. boneless country-style ribs
1/2 c. soy sauce
1/4 c. oil
1/4 c. onion, chopped
3 T. honey

3 T. dry sherry or water
2 t. fresh ginger, peeled
and grated
2 cloves garlic, minced

Place pork ribs in a large plastic zipping bag; set aside. Combine remaining ingredients in a bowl; mix well and pour over ribs. Seal bag; turn to coat. Refrigerate for several hours or overnight; drain. (If desired, bring marinade to a boil and brush over ribs.) Grill ribs on a hot grill to desired doneness. Serves 4.

Warm summer sun, shine kindly here.

–Mark Twain

Backyard Cookouts
& Easy Suppers

Grilled Chicken & Vegetables

Gloria Kaufmann
Orrville, OH

A healthy way to get your vegetables and protein!
Adjust this to your family's favorite veggies.

1/4 c. olive oil
2 T. balsamic vinegar
1 T. sugar
2 cloves garlic, minced
1/2 t. dried oregano
1/2 t. dried rosemary
1/4 t. salt
1/4 t. pepper

4 boneless, skinless chicken
   breasts
4 portabella mushrooms, sliced
1 red or yellow pepper, quartered
   or sliced
1 zucchini, halved
1 onion, sliced

In a large plastic zipping bag, combine olive oil, vinegar, sugar, garlic and seasonings; mix well. Add chicken and vegetables; seal bag and turn to coat evenly. Refrigerate for several hours, turning bag occasionally. Drain, discarding marinade. Arrange chicken and vegetables on a hot grill, placing vegetables in a grill pan, if desired. Grill about 5 to 6 minutes per side, until chicken is cooked through and vegetables are crisp-tender. Makes 4 servings.

Bundle together sprigs of fresh herbs like rosemary, thyme and marjoram with twine to create an herb basting brush. It really adds flavor to grilled foods!

Spring & Summer
Recipes for Sharing

Yummy Chicken Stir-Fry

Catherine Cherpes
Holland, MI

This recipe is the combination that I found most delicious after many times of making stir-fry over the years. Packed with garden-fresh veggies, it's perfect for a summer meal.

3 boneless, skinless
   chicken breasts
salt and pepper to taste
4 T. olive oil, divided
2 cloves garlic, minced
1 c. sliced mushrooms
1 to 2 yellow squash, quartered
   and chopped

1 red pepper, chopped
1 bunch green onions, chopped
2 carrots, peeled and chopped
1 to 2 stalks celery, chopped
1 bunch broccoli flowerets,
   chopped
stir-fry sauce to taste
cooked rice

Season chicken with salt and pepper. Heat 2 tablespoons olive oil in a skillet over medium heat. Add chicken and cook until tender and golden on both sides; drain. Remove chicken to a plate; let cool. Meanwhile, add remaining oil and garlic; cook for 30 seconds. Add vegetables; cook and stir over medium heat until crisp-tender. Shred chicken and return to pan. Increase heat to high; cook and stir quickly until edges are browned slightly. Toss with stir-fry sauce as desired. Serve chicken and vegetables over cooked rice. Makes 4 to 6 servings.

Grilled pineapple is a special summer treat! Great with chicken or pork...delicious with ice cream for dessert, too. Cut a fresh pineapple into wedges or rings. Brush with butter and sprinkle with brown sugar. Grill on both sides for 2 to 3 minutes, to desired doneness.

Backyard Cookouts
& Easy Suppers

Helen's Bows & Beef

Diane Himpelmann
Ringwood, IL

Back in the 1950s, my mom was one of the few women I knew who knew how to drive a car. She would drive a bunch of us girls to our overnight camp, and every time we'd ask her to bring "Bows." My friends still talk about this dish, and it's still a favorite in our home.

2 c. bowtie pasta, uncooked
1 lb. lean ground beef
1/4 c. onion, diced
14-3/4 oz. can corn, drained
1/2 t. garlic salt

salt and pepper to taste
10-3/4 oz. can tomato soup
1/2 c. plus 2 T. milk
1 c. shredded Cheddar cheese

Cook pasta according to package directions; drain. Meanwhile, brown beef with onion in a skillet over medium heat; drain. Add cooked pasta, corn and seasonings to beef; mix well. Whisk together soup and milk in a small bowl; add to beef mixture and stir well. Transfer mixture to a greased 13"x9" baking pan. Cover and bake at 350 degrees for 45 minutes. Uncover and top with cheese. Bake, uncovered, another 15 minutes. Makes 6 servings.

Remember to tote along some blankets or folding stools when you go camping. There's nothing like sitting around a glowing campfire swapping stories, stargazing and just enjoying time together with family & friends!

Spring & Summer
Recipes for Sharing

Ellen's Barbecued Spareribs

Daisy Sedalnick
Westminster, CO

My sister gave me this recipe when I had my first apartment,
way back in 1969. It's always a hit when I make it for
family & friends...it's delicious!

3 to 4 lbs. farmer-style or
    country-style pork ribs
1 lemon, thinly sliced
1 onion, thinly sliced
2 c. water

1 c. catsup
1/3 c. Worcestershire sauce
1/8 to 1/4 t. hot pepper sauce
1 t. chili powder
1 t. salt

Place ribs in a lightly greased shallow roasting pan, meaty side up.
Top each rib with a thin slice of lemon and a thin slice of onion. Bake,
uncovered, at 450 degrees for 30 minutes; reduce oven temperature
to 350 degrees. Meanwhile, stir together remaining ingredients in a
saucepan; bring to a boil over medium heat. Spoon sauce over ribs.
Continue baking at 350 degrees for about 45 minutes, until tender,
spooning sauce over ribs every 15 minutes. If sauce gets too thick,
stir in more water, 1/2 cup at a time. Makes 4 servings.

When serving sticky, saucy party foods like ribs and wings,
set out a basket of rolled-up fingertip towels, moistened with
lemon-scented water and warmed briefly in the microwave.
Such a thoughtful touch!

Backyard Cookouts
& Easy Suppers

Grilled Cheese Onion Burgers

Heather Porter
Villa Park, IL

I came up with this recipe one day when I started making burgers and didn't realize I was out of buns. Sourdough bread was a great substitute!

1 lb. ground beef chuck
1 T. fiesta ranch seasoning mix
1 t. pepper
softened butter to taste
8 slices sourdough bread
8 slices Pepper Jack cheese

1 sweet onion, sliced
salt and pepper to taste
Garnish: sliced beefsteak
 tomatoes, dill pickle slices
Optional: favorite burger
 condiments

Combine beef, seasoning mix and pepper in a bowl. Mix gently; form into 4 patties. Grill or pan-fry patties to medium doneness. Meanwhile, spread butter on one side of bread slices. Place all slices on a hot grill or griddle; grill until crisp and golden. Remove 4 bread slices; top remaining slices with 2 cheese slices each. Grill until cheese is melted; remove from grill. In a small skillet, sauté onion in a little more butter until soft and golden; season with salt and pepper. Assemble sandwiches with burgers, tomato slices, grilled onions, pickle slices and desired condiments. Makes 4 sandwiches.

Testing the heat on a charcoal grill or over a campfire is easy.
If you can hold your hand 5 inches over the coals for 2 to 3 seconds,
the coals are hot; 4 to 5 seconds means the coals are medium,
and a full 6 seconds means the heat is low.

Spring & Summer
Recipes for Sharing

Grilled Spanish Chicken Supper

Mary Garcia
Phoenix, AZ

*A delicious dinner, all in one! Serve with
steamed yellow rice, if desired.*

3 to 4 russet potatoes, peeled
    and cubed
14-1/2 oz. can diced tomatoes
    with roasted garlic
1 green pepper, chopped
1 red pepper, chopped
1 c. onion, coarsely chopped

1/2 c. sliced green olives with
    pimentos, drained
1 T. all-purpose flour
3 t. chili powder, divided
1 t. salt, divided
1-1/2 lbs. chicken breast tenders

In large bowl, combine potatoes, tomatoes with juice, peppers, onion
and olives. Stir in flour, 2 teaspoons chili powder and 1/2 teaspoon salt.
Spoon mixture onto an 18-inch by 15-inch piece of heavy-duty
aluminum foil; top with chicken tenders. Sprinkle chicken with
remaining salt and chili powder. Top with another piece of foil, the
same length; crimp foil all around to form a bag. Carefully place foil
bag on a heated grill. Grill, uncovered, over medium-high heat for about
20 minutes. Open carefully to check that chicken juices run clear and
potatoes are tender. Reseal bag and continue grilling, as necessary.
Open bag carefully and serve. Makes 4 servings.

If you love to cook out, but the weather isn't cooperative, pick up
a ridged cast-iron grill skillet. It's handy for grilling on the stovetop
whenever it's too cold or rainy to use the grill outdoors.

Backyard Cookouts
& Easy Suppers

Famous Fried Chicken

Joan Baker
Westland, MI

This is the only chicken recipe our family likes! My mom found this recipe in a doctor's waiting room magazine (of all places!) over 35 years ago.

1-1/2 c. all-purpose flour
1.9-oz. pkg. tomato soup mix
1.05-oz. pkg. Italian salad
   dressing mix
1-1/2 t. paprika

1/2 t. seasoning salt
3-1/2 lb. chicken, cut up,
   or 8 pieces chicken
1/4 c. butter, melted

In a large plastic zipping bag, combine flour, soup mix, dressing mix, paprika and salt. Shake well to combine thoroughly. Pat chicken pieces dry; add to mixture in bag and shake to coat well. Arrange chicken skin-side up in a 13"x9" baking pan sprayed with non-stick vegetable spray. Using a pastry brush, dab all of the melted butter over chicken. (Drizzling the butter does not work.) Bake, uncovered, at 350 degrees for one hour, or until chicken is tender and golden. Serves 4 to 5.

Serve fried chicken in clean new paper buckets from a local
paint store. Lined with red-checked paper napkins just
for fun, they're easy to toss when the picnic is over!

Grilled Veggie Pasta

Stephanie D'Esposito
Ravena, NY

This beautiful, healthy meatless dish is perfect for summer entertaining. It's also a great way to use up your garden surplus. If you don't have a grill pan, poke some holes in a disposable aluminum pan and set it right on the grill.

16-oz. pkg. penne pasta,
   uncooked
2 T. butter
1/4 c. grated Parmesan cheese
1/2 lb. asparagus, trimmed and
   cut into 1-inch pieces
1/2 lb. sliced mushrooms

2 small zucchini, thinly sliced
1 red pepper, sliced into
   1/2-inch strips
1 red onion, sliced
2 T. olive oil
1 t. salt
1/2 t. pepper

Cook pasta according to package directions; drain and return to pan. Toss pasta with butter and Parmesan cheese; cover and set aside. Meanwhile, combine all vegetables in a bowl; toss with olive oil, salt and pepper. Transfer vegetables to a grill pan; place on preheated grill. Grill over medium heat, stirring occasionally, for 15 to 20 minutes, until crisp-tender or cooked to desired doneness. Add vegetable mixture to pasta mixture; toss well and serve. Makes 6 servings.

Hickory, mesquite and applewood chips add wonderful
smoky flavor to grilled foods. Just soak in water,
drain and scatter onto hot coals.

Backyard Cookouts
& Easy Suppers

Blackened Shrimp

Roberta Simpkins
Mentor on the Lake, OH

This recipe has become a summertime staple in our household.
Serve with a big tossed salad and some crisp bread
to soak up the tasty juices.

1-1/2 lbs. large shrimp, peeled
   and cleaned
2 t. brown sugar, packed
1 T. chili powder
1 T. paprika
1 t. ground cumin

1 t. dried oregano
1 t. garlic powder
1 t. salt
1/2 t. pepper
1 to 2 t. olive oil
4 cloves garlic

Add shrimp to a large plastic zipping bag; set aside. Combine brown sugar and seasonings in a cup; sprinkle over shrimp and mix well. Seal bag and refrigerate for 30 to 60 minutes. Heat olive oil in a cast-iron skillet over medium-high heat. Add shrimp; cook for 2 minutes. Turn shrimp over; cook an additional 2 minutes. Scatter garlic over shrimp. Cook and stir for an additional 30 seconds and serve. Makes 2 to 3 servings.

Being from coastal Maine, we enjoy boating. When I was a kid, my whole family would pile into 3 or 4 boats and take a ride upriver to a small island for a 4th of July picnic. Coolers would be stuffed with lots of yummy salads, hot dogs, burgers and chips, plus plenty of fluffy blankets, chairs and swimsuits, of course. And fresh watermelon for dessert! Late in the afternoon, only the incoming tide would force us to leave for home. I have so many pictures and fond memories of our time on that little island each July.

–Lisa Cunningham, Boothbay, ME

Spring & Summer
Recipes for Sharing

Griddle Burger Sandwiches

Nancy Kailihiwa
Wheatland, CA

This is one of our family's all-time favorite sandwiches! We cook it on the griddle outside. It can easily be made in a skillet as well.

1 lb. lean ground beef
4 T. butter, divided
1 T. Worcestershire sauce
1-1/2 t. pepper, garlic & herb
   seasoning blend
1/2 onion, sliced and separated
   into rings

12 slices thick-sliced Texas toast,
   divided
6 slices Colby Jack cheese
Optional: catsup, mustard
   and/or fry sauce

Heat an outdoor griddle over medium-high heat. To one section of griddle, add beef and 1-1/2 tablespoons butter; break up beef into large crumbles. Sprinkle with Worcestershire sauce and seasoning blend. To another section of griddle, add onion rings and another 1-1/2 tablespoons butter. Cook until beef is browned and onion rings are soft and mostly translucent. Mix together beef and onion; continue cooking. Melt remaining butter and brush over 6 slices bread. Place bread on griddle, butter-side down; reduce heat to low under bread. Top each bread slice with one cheese slice; spoon beef mixture over cheese. Top with remaining bread. Continue cooking and flipping until sandwiches are golden on both sides. Serve with desired condiments. Makes 6 sandwiches.

Hot honey adds zest to grilled meats, veggies, even biscuits!
Find it in the condiment aisle, or to make it yourself, combine
one cup clover honey, 2 sliced fresh hot peppers and one dried red
chile in a saucepan. Simmer over low heat for 10 minutes; cool.
Strain and bottle honey.

Backyard Cookouts
& Easy Suppers

Camping Cowboy Hot Dogs

Bev Traxler
British Columbia, Canada

A camping favorite! Save time by preparing all the ingredients at home to pack in the cooler. Serve with baked beans and potato chips...yummy!

10 slices bacon, crisply cooked
   and crumbled
1/2 c. onion, chopped
1/2 c. shredded Cheddar cheese

1/4 c. barbecue sauce
8 hot dogs
8 hot dog buns, split

Before traveling to campsite, pack crumbled bacon, onion, cheese and barbecue sauce in individual containers. Roast hot dogs over a campfire or grill. To serve, spread barbecue sauce on each bun; add a roasted hot dog. Top with crumbled bacon, cheese and onion. Makes 8 sandwiches.

Gourmet Hot Dogs

Charlene McCain
Bakersfield, CA

Who doesn't love hot dogs? Perk up your puppies by boiling them first, then grilling in a skillet. Add the condiments suggested, or pile on your own favorites.

8 hot dogs
8 hot dog buns, split

mustard and pickle relish to taste
1 red onion, diced

In a saucepan of boiling water, cook hot dogs until plump; drain. Split hot dogs almost in half lengthwise. Add hot dogs to a hot skillet; cook on each side for about one minute, until beginning to crisp and blacken. (Hold hot dogs flat with a spatula, if necessary.) Remove from skillet. Open hot dog buns flat and add to skillet, cut-side down. Cook until edges crisp slightly. Spread mustard on one side of bun, pickle relish on the other. Place a hot dog in center of bun; sprinkle with onion and serve. Serves 8.

Spring & Summer
Recipes for Sharing

Real Deal Carne Asada

Becky Butler
Keller, TX

We love Tex-Mex food here in Texas, and this is my go-to recipe for grilled beef. Resting is essential for juicy, tender beef, so don't skip that step. This is the real deal! Include the jalapeño seeds if you like more heat.

1 c. fresh cilantro, chopped
1/4 c. olive oil
4 cloves garlic, minced
1 jalapeño pepper, seeded
   and minced
1/2 c. orange juice
zest and juice of 2 limes

2 T. vinegar
1/2 t. ground cumin
1/2 t. salt
1/2 t. pepper
2 lbs. beef flank steak, sirloin
   flap or skirt steak

In a one-gallon plastic zipping bag, combine all ingredients except steak; mix well. Add steak to bag; toss to coat. Refrigerate at least 3 hours or overnight. Heat a grill to high heat. Lay steak flat on grill, discarding marinade in bag. Do not move steak for 7 to 10 minutes, depending on desired doneness. When well caramelized on first side, flip steak over; grill another 7 to 10 minutes. Remove to a cutting board; cover with aluminum foil and let rest 15 minutes. Slice steak across the grain into very thin strips; serve as desired. Makes 4 to 6 servings.

Fajitas: fill warm flour tortillas with steak strips. Top with grilled onions and peppers, sour cream, guacamole and shredded Cheddar cheese.

Street tacos: fill warm corn tortillas with steak strips. Top with diced onion, chopped fresh cilantro, crumbled queso fresco and a lime wedge.

Liven up summer beverages by adding frozen slices of lemon or lime, for a refreshing hint of citrus.

Backyard Cookouts
& Easy Suppers

Enchilada Casserole

Shannon Harper
San Antonio, TX

This recipe is fast, easy and popular...it always disappears at potlucks! I prefer ground venison and extra-sharp Cheddar.

1 lb. ground venison or beef
19-oz. can red enchilada sauce
10 6-inch corn tortillas, torn into large pieces and divided

1 onion, chopped and divided
8-oz. pkg. shredded extra-sharp Cheddar cheese, divided
1-1/2 c. water

Brown venison or beef in a skillet over medium heat; drain. Stir in enchilada sauce; remove from heat. Spread half of tortilla pieces evenly in a lightly greased 13"x9" baking pan. Layer with half of venison mixture, half of onion and half of cheese. Repeat layers. Pour water over all; cover tightly with aluminum foil. Bake at 400 degrees for 30 minutes. Makes 8 servings.

Make copies of favorite time-tested recipes to share when family & friends are getting together. Invite others to bring their recipes to share too. It's a great way to preserve them and bring back the sweetest memories.

Spring & Summer
Recipes for Sharing

Aloha Chicken

Hollie Moots
Marysville, OH

This marinade is simple, but makes the best grilled chicken. It grills up nice and juicy! It's perfect for a cookout with family...maybe grill some fresh pineapple alongside the chicken, too!

10 to 12 boneless, skinless
   chicken breasts or thighs
1 c. brown sugar, packed
3/4 c. catsup
1/2 c. soy sauce

1/4 c. pineapple juice
1/4 c. chicken broth
2 t. fresh ginger, peeled
   and minced
1 t. garlic, minced

Place chicken in a large plastic zipping bag; set aside. Combine remaining ingredients in a bowl; mix well and spoon over chicken. Seal bag and refrigerate for 8 hours or overnight, turning bag occasionally. Drain; discard marinade. Grill chicken over medium-low heat for about 5 to 7 minutes per side, until chicken juices run clear. Makes 10 to 12 servings.

Slow-Cooker Saucy Cola Pulled Pork

Marietta Hayter
Midland, TX

This is a quick & easy meal that my family loves. I like to use honey barbecue sauce, but you can use any flavor you like. I serve the pork on dinner yeast rolls, topped with coleslaw or cheese to make the perfect sliders. Other times, we roll in a flour tortilla and make burritos...very tasty!

3-1/2 lb. boneless pork shoulder
   roast, trimmed
19-oz. bottle honey barbecue
   sauce

12-oz. can cola beverage
Optional: dinner rolls, split,
   or flour tortillas

Place roast in a 6-quart slow cooker; top with barbecue sauce and cola. Cover and cook on low setting for 8 to 10 hours, until roast shreds easily. Transfer roast to a cutting board; shred. Stir shredded pork back into sauce and serve as desired. Serves 6 to 8.

Backyard Cookouts
& Easy Suppers

Scott's Chicken & Summer Fruit Kabobs

Carolyn Deckard
Bedford, IN

My son in-law makes these delicious kabobs for us every July 4th while camping. He always doubles the recipe, especially when having guests show up, which we enjoy.

1 lb. boneless, skinless chicken breast, cut into 1-1/2 inch cubes
2 ripe peaches or nectarines, pitted and cut into 1-inch wedges
2 ripe plums, pitted and cut into 1-inch wedges
1/2 c. peach or apricot jam
1/2 t. salt

Spray grill rack with non-stick vegetable spray; heat coals or grill for direct heat. Alternately thread chicken, peaches and plums onto 6 skewers, leaving some space between pieces. In a cup, mix jam with salt. Place kabobs on grill over medium heat, 4 to 5 inches from heat. Grill for 15 to 20 minutes, turning occasionally and brushing with jam, until chicken is no longer pink in center. Serves 6.

There's always such great food at block parties that we all want to try a bit of everything! To help out, try making bite-size burgers, and cut wooden skewers in half for mini kabobs...perfect!

Spring & Summer
Recipes for Sharing

Glazed Picnic Loaf

Bev Traxler
British Columbia, Canada

This meatloaf is a family favorite. It keeps well and slices beautifully. It can be served immediately, or chilled and served for sandwiches.

1 lb. lean ground beef
3/4 c. onion, chopped
1/2 c. milk
1 egg, beaten
8 saltine crackers, crushed
salt and pepper to taste

1/4 c. brown sugar, packed
1/4 c. catsup
1/4 c. golden syrup or light
  corn syrup
1 t. dry mustard

In a large bowl, combine beef, onion, milk, egg, crackers, salt and pepper; mix well and shape into a loaf. Place in an ungreased 9"x5" loaf pan; use a spoon to make a groove down the center of loaf. Combine remaining ingredients in another bowl; spoon over loaf. Bake, uncovered, at 350 degrees for one hour. Drain; remove from pan and slice. Makes 6 to 8 servings.

Family reunions are a summertime favorite...good food, family, laughter and memories in the making. Set the date early, at least 2 to 3 months in advance. This allows everyone plenty of time to plan for vacations, summer camp, weddings and any other activities.

Backyard Cookouts
& Easy Suppers

Stir-Fry Spaghetti

Denise Herr
West Jefferson, OH

My mom found this recipe in the newspaper back in the 1980s. It's so easy, light and delicious! I especially love to make it in the summer with fresh-picked cherry tomatoes. Instead of beef, you could use all chicken or shrimp...even make it meatless.

1 lb. beef sirloin steak, cut
   into strips
2 cloves garlic, minced
1 T. extra-virgin olive oil
salt and pepper to taste
2 small zucchini, diced

1 c. cherry tomatoes, halved
1/4 c. zesty Italian salad dressing
2 c. cooked thin spaghetti
1 T. grated Parmesan cheese
Garnish: chopped fresh basil
   or parsley

In a skillet over medium heat, sauté beef and garlic in oil for one to 1-1/2 minutes. Drain; season with salt and pepper. Remove beef mixture to a plate; cover to keep warm. Add zucchini to skillet and sauté for 2 to 3 minutes, until crisp-tender. Add tomatoes; cook for one more minute. Add salad dressing; return beef to skillet and stir to combine. Add cooked spaghetti and heat through. At serving time, top with Parmesan cheese and herbs as desired. Makes 3 to 4 servings.

When chopping ingredients, be sure not to cut uncooked meat and fresh veggies on the same cutting board. Keep 2 cutting boards on hand...no need to stop and wash one before continuing.

Spring & Summer
Recipes for Sharing

Pat's Chicken Teriyaki Burgers

Pat Martin
Riverside, CA

Back in the late 1980s, our family loved the chicken teriyaki burgers served at our favorite burger joint. So I created a knock-off burger that had some healthier choices. A great burger for family or company!

4 boneless, skinless chicken
    breasts
10-oz. bottle teriyaki marinade
    & sauce
15-1/2 oz. can pineapple slices
    in juice, drained and 4 t. juice
    reserved

1/4 c. mayonnaise-style salad
    dressing
4 t. low-sodium soy sauce
4 hamburger buns, split
Garnish: iceberg lettuce, 8 tomato
    slices, 4 red onion slices,
    4 Swiss cheese slices

Place chicken breasts in a large plastic zipping bag; add enough teriyaki marinade to cover. Seal bag and refrigerate for one hour. Drain; discard marinade. Arrange chicken breasts on a hot grill; cook on both sides until golden and juices run clear. Meanwhile, mix reserved pineapple juice, salad dressing and soy sauce; spread on buns. Top each bottom bun with 2 pineapple slices, lettuce, 2 tomato slices and one onion slice. Add one chicken breast, one cheese slice and top bun. Makes 4 sandwiches.

Pick up a stack of retro-style plastic burger baskets. Lined with checked paper napkins, they're lots of fun for serving burgers, hot dogs and fries...and clean-up is a snap!

Backyard Cookouts
& Easy Suppers

Portabella Mushroom Burgers

Karen Davis
Glendale, AZ

*I make these at family cookouts for my daughter, who's a
vegetarian. Sometimes my husband has one, too!*

4 portabella mushroom caps	1 T. minced garlic
3 T. olive oil, divided	salt and pepper to taste
1/4 c. balsamic vinegar	4 slices provolone cheese
1 t. dried basil	4 whole-wheat sandwich
1 t. dried oregano	buns, split

Place mushroom caps right-side up in a shallow bowl. In another bowl,
whisk together 2 tablespoons oil, vinegar and seasonings. Spoon over
mushrooms; let stand for 15 minutes, turning twice. Brush grill with
remaining oil. Drain mushrooms, reserving marinade; place mushrooms
on grill over medium-high heat. Grill for 5 to 8 minutes per side, until
tender, brushing often with marinade. Top with cheese during the last
2 minutes of grilling. Serve on sandwich buns. Makes 4 sandwiches.

Zucchini Po' Boys

Francine Corter
Chicago, IL

A tasty way to enjoy all those zucchini.

1 T. butter	4 Italian sandwich rolls, split
2 to 3 zucchini, cubed	1 c. favorite marinara sauce
1/4 t. red pepper flakes	1-1/2 c. shredded mozzarella
salt and pepper to taste	cheese

Melt butter in a skillet over medium heat. Add zucchini; cook until
tender and golden. Sprinkle with seasonings. Spoon a generous amount
of zucchini mixture into each sandwich roll. Cover each with 1/4 cup
marinara sauce and a handful of cheese. Close rolls; wrap each roll with
aluminum foil. Bake at 350 degrees for 15 minutes, or until heated
through and cheese is melted. Serves 4.

Grill or toast buns sandwich buns before filling. It only takes
a moment and makes such a tasty difference!

Spring & Summer
Recipes for Sharing

Mom's BBQ Chicken

Emily Doody
Kentwood, MI

This is my husband's and kids' favorite barbecue chicken! We go back to it all grilling season. Chicken thighs are my favorite because they don't dry out easily. Chicken breasts can always be subbed, though. Serve with your favorite summer sides.

8 boneless, skinless chicken thighs	1/2 c. brown sugar, packed
1-1/2 c. sweet onion barbecue sauce	1 t. steak seasoning
	1/2 t. red pepper flakes
	1 T. cider vinegar

Place chicken thighs in a large plastic container or bowl; set aside. In another bowl, combine barbecue sauce, brown sugar, steak seasoning and red pepper flakes; reserve half of mixture for later. To the remaining half, add vinegar; spoon over chicken. Toss to coat evenly; cover and refrigerate up to 12 hours. Refrigerate reserved sauce mixture separately. Shortly before serving, drain chicken, discarding sauce mixture. Arrange chicken on oiled grill over medium heat. Cook for 5 minutes per side. Brush chicken with reserved sauce on both sides; reduce heat to medium-low. Continue to cook for about 10 more minutes, turning occasionally, until done and a meat thermometer inserted in the thickest part reads 165 degrees. Serve chicken with reserved sauce. Makes 8 servings.

Let the kids invite a special friend or 2 home on a cookout night. Keep it simple with grilled chicken or burgers and a crisp salad. A great way to get to know your children's playmates!

Backyard Cookouts
& Easy Suppers

Tender Pork Chops

Carrie Kelderman
Pella, IA

This is a wonderfully tender way to serve pork chops. My husband often grills on Sundays after church...this is a family favorite!

3 c. water
1/4 c. brown sugar, packed
1/4 c. salt

2 c. ice cubes
4 pork chops

Mix together water, brown sugar, salt and ice cubes in a large container with a lid. Add pork chops to brine. Cover and refrigerate for 3 to 4 hours. Discard brine. Grill as desired. Makes 4 servings.

Grilled Honey-Glazed Chicken

Nola Coons
Gooseberry Patch

Simple to fix...simply delicious!

4 boneless, skinless chicken
   thighs
2 T. olive oil
1/4 t. salt

1/4 t. pepper
1/4 c. honey
2 T. soy sauce
2 cloves garlic, minced

Brush chicken thighs with oil; season with salt and pepper. In a small bowl, whisk together honey, soy sauce and garlic; set aside. Arrange chicken on grill over medium heat. Cover and grill for 8 to 12 minutes, turning once and brushing with honey mixture in last 2 minutes, until juices run clear and a meat thermometer inserted in thickest part reads 165 degrees. Serves 4.

Spring & Summer
Recipes for Sharing

Grilled Chicken & Orzo Pasta
Liz Plotnick-Snay
Gooseberry Patch

We like to make this recipe in the summer, when we can grill outdoors. Using pre-grilled chicken from the freezer section makes it a light, quick & easy meal year 'round, too.

2 boneless, skinless chicken
   breasts
2 T. barbecue rub
14-oz. can low-sodium
   chicken broth

1 c. whole-wheat or plain orzo
   pasta, uncooked
1 pt. cherry tomatoes, halved
4-oz. can diced green chiles
2 t. ground cumin

Coat chicken with barbecue rub. Grill chicken on a hot grill for about 4 minutes per side, until done; set aside to cool. (Omit this step if using pre-grilled chicken.) In a large saucepan over high heat, stir together remaining ingredients; bring to a boil just briefly. Transfer mixture to a greased 2-quart casserole dish. Cut chicken into strips or cubes; arrange on top of orzo mixture. Cover and bake at 350 degrees for 20 minutes, or until orzo is tender. Cover and let stand for 10 minutes. Serves 3 to 4.

Pitch a tent in the backyard on a summer night so the kids
can camp out, tell ghost stories and play flashlight tag.
What a great way to make memories!

142

Backyard Cookouts
& Easy Suppers

Joneses' Cube Steaks & Beans

Lynnette Jones
East Flat Rock, NC

This is an old, old recipe of my husband's family. Always cooked on an outdoor brick stove over a fire on July 4th.

4 beef cube steaks
salt and pepper to taste
3 to 4 T. oil

1/2 c. onion, chopped
15-oz. can pork & beans

Season steaks with salt and pepper; set aside. Heat oil in a large cast-iron skillet over medium heat; add steaks. Cook for 2 to 3 minutes per side, until browned and cooked to desired doneness. Remove steaks to a serving plate; cover to keep warm. Add onion to drippings in skillet; cook until tender. Stir in pork & beans; simmer until beans are thickened and bubbly. Makes 4 servings.

Bratwurst Fajitas

Nikki Furey
Mendon, MI

I first made these fajitas while camping...now I make them for lots of gatherings. Yummy and easy to make.

2 to 3 T. oil
19-oz. pkg. bratwursts, sliced
1 green pepper, sliced
1 red pepper, sliced

1 red onion, sliced
6 to 8 flour tortillas, warmed
Garnish: spicy ranch sauce or
  sour cream

Heat a cast-iron skillet on grill over medium-high heat until hot. Add oil, bratwursts and vegetables. Cook until vegetables are tender and bratwursts are no longer pink in in the center. Serve with warm tortillas and favorite toppings. Serves 3 to 4.

Spring & Summer
Recipes for Sharing

Grilled Pork Tenderloin & Vegetables

Wendy Meadows
Spring Hill, FL

*I love to make this recipe when we have friends over
and it is just too hot to cook inside.*

1 to 2-lb. pork tenderloin
1 t. seasoning salt, or to taste
1 t. pepper
1/2 t. adobo seasoning
1 green pepper, cut into chunks
1 red pepper, cut into chunks

1 red onion, quartered, with
  root end intact
1 sweet potato, peeled and
  thinly sliced
1 T. extra-virgin olive oil
salt and pepper to taste

Sprinkle pork tenderloin with seasonings. Preheat grill to medium-high heat. Place tenderloin on grill over direct heat; cook for 3 to 5 minutes per side. Move tenderloin to indirect heat; cook until a meat thermometer inserted in thickest part reads 145 degrees. Set aside tenderloin on a platter; cover to keep warm. Drizzle all vegetables with olive oil; season with salt and pepper. Add onion and peppers to direct heat on grill. Cook for 5 minutes, or until charred; continue cooking over indirect heat for 2 to 3 minutes per side. Add sweet potatoes to direct heat. Cook over medium-high heat for 3 to 4 minutes per side, until charred. Cook over indirect heat for 2 minutes. Slice tenderloin; serve with vegetables. Makes 4 to 6 servings.

An old oven rack makes a handy grate for cooking over
a campfire. Simply prop it on several logs or large stones.

Backyard Cookouts
& Easy Suppers

Cindy's Camping Casserole

Cindy Slawski
Medford Lakes, NJ

I have so many great memories of eating this dish in the woods on camping trips around a campfire. But it's great for an easy and filling weeknight meal at home, too. It is quick to make and versatile. Leftovers freeze well too. Remember to follow it up with s'mores!

16-oz. pkg. bowtie pasta,
  uncooked
1/2 lb. sliced mushrooms
1 T. butter or olive oil
1 lb. ground beef or turkey

1 to 2 12-oz. jars favorite beef
  or brown gravy
garlic powder, salt and pepper
  to taste

Cook pasta according to package directions; drain. Meanwhile, in a large skillet over medium heat, cook mushrooms in butter or olive oil until tender. Add beef or turkey to skillet; cook until browned and drain. Stir in one jar gravy; add remaining jar, if desired. Add seasonings; cook and stir until gravy is heated through. Spoon gravy mixture over pasta and serve. Makes 4 to 6 servings.

When it's just too hot outside, serve up a salad buffet! Try a grilled chicken salad, a pasta salad, a crisp green tossed salad and a fruity gelatin salad. Crusty bread and a simple dessert complete a tasty, light meal that's sure to be enjoyed.

Spring & Summer
Recipes for Sharing

Beachfront Crab Cakes

Wendy Paffenroth
Pine Island, NY

Serve these seaside treats with cocktail sauce, a tossed salad and bread sticks. May be reheated on a baking sheet.

1 lb. crabmeat, thawed if frozen and flaked
1 egg, beaten
8 to 12 regular or whole-wheat buttery round crackers, crushed
1 to 2 t. green or red hot pepper sauce
2 to 3 sprigs fresh parsley, snipped
1/8 t. pepper
1/4 c. onion, diced
2 to 3 T. mayonnaise
canola or olive oil for frying
Optional: paprika

Place crabmeat in a large bowl; pick through and remove any shells. Add egg, crackers, hot sauce, parsley and pepper; mix well. Add onion; stir in mayonnaise. Dampen your hands with cold water to prevent sticking; form crab mixture into 15 to 20 small balls. In a skillet over medium heat, heat just enough oil to cover. Add crab cakes and cook until golden, turning often. Remove to paper towels to drain. May also arrange in a greased 13"x9" baking pan. Bake, uncovered, at 325 degrees for 20 to 30 minutes. If desired, sprinkle with paprika. Makes 4 to 5 servings.

Host a backyard beach party! Toss colorful beach towels over the tables. Serve up grilled shrimp or crab cakes and cool salads, with snacks heaped in plastic buckets from the dollar store. Fun in the sun!

146

Backyard Cookouts
& Easy Suppers

Orange-Glazed Salmon

Courtney Stultz
Weir, KS

My family requested a new recipe to enjoy during Lent and I wanted something with salmon. So, I began searching the pantry for something to give it a twist. I saw some orange marmalade and had my doubts, but the sweet citrus flavor paired so well with the spice blend. It was a huge hit at our house and will definitely be enjoyed all year long!

4 4-oz. salmon fillets
1 t. sesame seed
1/2 t. red pepper flakes
1/2 t. ground ginger
1/2 t. garlic powder
1/2 t. onion powder

1/2 t. sea salt
1/2 t. pepper
1/2 c. orange marmalade
5 T. reduced-sodium soy sauce
2 t. Dijon mustard

Arrange salmon fillets skin-side down in a lightly greased aluminum foil-lined 13"x9" baking pan; set aside. Combine all seasonings in a cup; sprinkle over salmon. Mix remaining ingredients in another cup. Top each fillet with a spoonful of mixture. Bake, uncovered, at 375 degrees for 12 to 15 minutes, until salmon is cooked through and flakes easily with a fork. Serves 4.

Shall I compare thee to a summer's day?
Thou art more lovely and more temperate.
–William Shakespeare

Spring & Summer
Recipes for Sharing

Grilled Chicken Adobo

Lynda Hart
Bluffdale, UT

It's fun to grill in the early evening as summer temperatures drop a little. You can make the ordinary into extraordinary by putting out lanterns, torches and strings of lights. It then becomes a magical occasion for your guests!

1/2 c. onion, coarsely chopped
6 cloves garlic
1/3 c. lime juice
1 t. dried oregano
1 t. ground cumin
1/2 t. dried thyme
1/4 t. cayenne pepper
6 boneless, skinless chicken breasts
3 T. fresh cilantro, chopped

Combine onion, garlic and lime juice in a food processor; process until finely minced. Transfer to a large plastic zipping bag; add seasonings. Knead bag to mix; add chicken breasts to bag. Seal bag, pressing out the air. Refrigerate for one to 4 hours, occasionally turning bag. Transfer chicken to greased grill, discarding onion mixture. Grill for 5 to 7 minutes per side, until no longer pink. Transfer to a serving plate; garnish with cilantro and serve. Makes 6 servings.

To celebrate Fathers' Day, fill a basket with jars of barbecue sauce, gourmet mustard, pickles and relish...a great gift for anyone who loves summertime grilling. Tuck in a set of tongs, an apron and favorite grilling cookbook. Sure to be a hit with Dad!

Backyard Cookouts
& Easy Suppers

One-Pot Taco Pasta

Nancy Kailihiwa
Wheatland, CA

My kids love this dish! It travels well and is great for church picnics and potlucks. Pair it with a tossed salad for a complete meal. For extra spice, use Mexican-blend cheese.

1 lb. ground beef
1 onion, chopped
1-oz. pkg. taco seasoning mix
4 c. beef broth
2 c. milk

16-oz. pkg. penne pasta, uncooked
8-oz. pkg. shredded Cheddar cheese

Brown beef with onion in a large skillet over medium heat; drain. Add taco seasoning, beef broth and milk; stir well. Add uncooked pasta; stir well. Bring to a boil over high heat; reduce heat to medium. Simmer for 9 to 12 minutes until pasta is cooked, stirring occasionally. Stir in cheese; let stand for 5 minutes before serving. Serves 10.

When my brother Virgie and I were kids growing up in the small rural community of Blue Ball in southwest Arkansas, we couldn't wait for summertime. Summers meant fishing in Dutch Creek and swimming in the Blue Hole. We kept our cane poles, hooks and line down at the creek, and of course, our worm bucket. We would dig our worms on the creek bank, then spend wonderful hours fishing. When we got too hot, sometimes we'd just jump in and swim awhile. I love to remember those precious memories and think of a way of life that is long gone.

–Beckie Apple, Grannis, AR

Spring & Summer
Recipes for Sharing

Honey Balsamic Chicken

Tammy Griffin
Ontario, Canada

This has become one of our summertime staples! We love to use the slow cooker when we're camping in our trailer. Serve with rice.

10 to 12 chicken drumsticks or
   thighs, skin removed
1/2 c. balsamic vinegar
1/2 c. honey

1/2 c. brown sugar, packed
1/4 c. soy sauce
5 cloves garlic, minced

Arrange chicken drumsticks in a 6-quart slow cooker; set aside. Combine remaining ingredients in a small bowl; stir until brown sugar is dissolved. Spoon over chicken in crock. Cover and cook on low setting for 4 to 6 hours, or on high setting for 3 to 4 hours. Makes 10 to 12 servings.

Asian Beef Kabobs

Paige Bear
Lyman, SC

My family loves steak, and this marinade combines two of our favorite sauces! This recipe doubles or triples easily!

1/3 c. Worcestershire sauce
1/3 c. hoisin sauce
1 T. steak seasoning

1 lb. beef top sirloin, fat trimmed,
   cut into one-inch cubes

Combine sauces and seasoning in a large plastic zipping bag; mix well. Add steak cubes to bag; seal bag and turn to coat. Refrigerate for 4 to 6 hours, turning bag occasionally. Divide steak cubes among 4 skewers. Place a double thickness of heavy-duty aluminum foil on grill heated to 350 degrees. Arrange kabobs on foil. Close lid; grill kabobs for 3 minutes per side. Serves 4.

In hot, humid weather, keep salt free-flowing by placing a few dry grains of rice in the shaker.

Backyard Cookouts
& Easy Suppers

Sticky Burgers

Gayla Reyes
Fairfield, OH

This is a new craze around my hometown. I make pepper jellies to sell, and many of my customers who purchase the jelly tell me it's for this recipe! It's an odd combination, but so yummy. Delicious!

4 ground beef patties
4 hamburger buns, split
   and toasted
peanut butter to taste

4 slices Pepper Jack cheese
jalapeño pepper jelly to taste
Garnish: sliced tomatoes and
   onions, lettuce leaves

Grill or pan-fry patties as desired. On each bottom bun, layer peanut butter, a burger, a cheese slice and pepper jelly. Add tomatoes, onions and lettuce as desired; add top buns and serve. Makes 4 sandwiches.

Sunny Bacon Burgers

Amy Thomason Hunt
Traphill, NC

This is a great variation on the plain burger...it goes well with a Hawaiian-themed cookout.

1-1/2 to 2 lbs. ground beef
1/2 c. barbecue sauce
garlic salt to taste
pepper to taste

4 pineapple rings
8 slices bacon, crisply cooked
Optional: additional barbecue
   sauce

Combine beef, barbecue sauce and seasonings. Mix well; form into 4 patties. On a hot grill, cook to desired doneness. On each bottom bun, place a burger, a pineapple ring and 2 slices of bacon; add additional sauce, if desired. Add top bun and serve. Makes 4 sandwiches.

Delicious burgers begin with ground beef chuck labeled as 80/20. A little fat in the beef adds flavor...there's no need to purchase ground sirloin.

Spring & Summer
Recipes for Sharing

Backyard Mustard BBQ Sauce

Vivian Marshall
Columbus, OH

A very perfect barbecue sauce for burgers, steaks, ribs or even just off the spoon! Our family likes sauces with a kick, so this one has been tweaked by my daughter and me to satisfy our taste buds. I like to use kimchi catsup in it for the kick.

1/2 c. Dijon mustard	2 T. light brown sugar, packed
1/2 c. yellow mustard	1 T. Worcestershire sauce
1/4 c. molasses	1 t. pepper
1/4 c. cider vinegar	Optional: 1 T. hot pepper sauce
3 T. catsup	

Combine all ingredients in a saucepan over medium heat and mix well. Bring to a boil; reduce heat to low. Simmer for 15 minutes, stirring occasionally, just until slightly thickened. Remove from heat and serve; refrigerate leftovers. The longer sauce stands, the more the flavors blend. Makes about 2 cups.

If it's been too long since you've visited with good friends, why not host a casual get-together? Potlucks are so easy to plan...everyone brings along their favorite dish to share. It's all about food, fun and fellowship!

Backyard Cookouts
& Easy Suppers

Bobby Rae's Old Alabama
White Sauce

Staci Prickett
Montezuma, GA

Use this delicious sauce on grilled ribs, pulled pork and burgers, in potato salads, coleslaw and deviled eggs too. One traditional way to use this sauce is to dunk your grilled or smoked chicken until wholly submerged, remove and allow the chicken to rest a few minutes before serving. Yummy! Be sure to use the best mayonnaise and buttermilk!

1/3 c. mayonnaise
3 T. buttermilk
3 T. cider vinegar
1 T. white or brown sugar, packed
1/2 t. prepared horseradish
1/4 t. paprika

1/4 t. garlic powder
1/4 t. dry mustard
1/8 t. onion powder
1/8 t. cayenne pepper
1/2 t. salt
1/4 t. pepper

Combine all ingredients in a bowl; whisk until smooth and well combined. Cover and refrigerate for a few hours before serving, or overnight for the best flavor. Makes 1-1/4 cups.

Send cookout guests home with jars of your very own, secret-recipe grilling sauce...sure to be a hit!

Spring & Summer
Recipes for Sharing

Beer Batter Fish

Kathryn Benkow
East Aurora, NY

During Lent, I use this recipe every Friday for dinner. It is my husband's favorite meal. The recipe was passed down to me by my aunt, and I will be forever grateful. Serve with crisp golden home fries and coleslaw...enjoy!

2 c. biscuit baking mix or all-
  purpose flour, divided
12-oz. can beer
3 egg whites

salt and pepper to taste
1 lb. haddock fillets, thawed
  if frozen
oil for frying

In a bowl, stir together 1-1/2 cups baking mix or flour and beer; let stand at room temperature for several hours, until bubbly. Beat egg whites with an electric mixer on high speed until stiff peaks form; fold into baking mixture. Season with salt and pepper. Dredge fish fillets in remaining baking mix or flour; add to batter and coat on both sides. Heat 1/4-inch oil in a skillet over medium-high heat. Add fillets and cook for 8 minutes per side. Serves 2 to 3.

Captain Chuck's Famous Tartar Sauce

Karen Antonides
Gahanna, OH

My husband loves to fish and and to prepare his catch for family & friends. This tangy tartar sauce prepared from a family recipe is enjoyed by all who taste it. Many folks say it's the best they have ever had!

1 c. mayonnaise-type salad
  dressing
1/2 to 3/4 c. Thousand Island
  salad dressing

2 T. dill pickle relish
2 T. dill pickle juice
1/4 t. Worcestershire sauce

Mix together all ingredients, adjusting any ingredients to taste. Cover and store in the refrigerator. Makes 10 servings.

Sunny-Day
Gatherings

Spring & Summer
Recipes for Sharing

Hot Dog Dippin' Nuggets

Lisa Staib
Tumbling Shoals, AR

We like to put together some of our summer favorites...great finger foods, easy nibbling with toothpicks too. Just grab a handful of nuggets and fries...dip away! Tasty with ice-cold lemonade and dill pickles on the side.

1 to 2 16-oz. pkgs. frozen
    seasoned crinkle fries or
    potato wedges
salt and pepper to taste
6 to 8 beef hot dogs, cut
    into thirds

16-oz. container bacon &
    cheddar sour cream dip
16-oz. jar favorite salsa
15-oz. can nacho Cheddar cheese
    sauce, warmed

Bake frozen potatoes according to package instructions; season with salt and pepper. Meanwhile, grill or broil hot dog pieces for 2 to 5 minutes, turning occasionally. To serve, heap fries and nuggets into dinner baskets or plates. Serve with sauces for dipping. Serves 4 to 8.

Old-fashioned wooden cutting boards in fun shapes like pigs,
fish or roosters can often be found at tag sales. Put them
to use as whimsical party snack servers.

Sunny-Day *Gatherings*

BLT Pinwheels

Karen Wilson
Defiance, OH

*I always have some leftover tortillas after my grandkids visit.
This is a great way to use them up. I like the tomato-flavored
tortillas best for this.*

1/2 c. mayonnaise
1/2 c. cream cheese, softened
2 T. thick and chunky salsa
1 t. Dijon mustard
6 slices bacon, crisply cooked
   and crumbled

3 8-inch or 10-inch flour tortillas
1 c. roma tomatoes, chopped
1-1/2 c. romaine lettuce,
   shredded

Combine mayonnaise, cream cheese, salsa and mustard in a small bowl.
Stir until blended; fold in bacon. Spread bacon mixture evenly over
tortillas; top with tomatoes and lettuce. Tightly roll up tortillas and
wrap in plastic wrap. Refrigerate for at least one hour, but not more
than 6 hours. Cut into one-inch slices; secure each slice with a
toothpick. Serves 8 to 10.

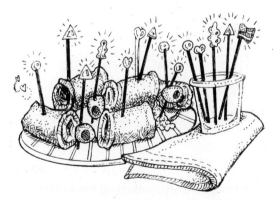

Dress up roll-ups and other finger foods with seasonal
party picks...makes a party platter look extra special in a jiffy!
Add a small olive or pickled pepper for extra pizzazz.

Spring & Summer
Recipes for Sharing

Rebecca's Famous Salsa

Marta Norton
Redlands, CA

I always keep this salsa on hand. Not only is it good for snacking...
it adds so much great flavor to all of my Mexican dishes!

1 jalapeño pepper, halved
1 Red Fresno pepper, halved
28-oz. can peeled whole
   tomatoes
7-oz. can Mexican salsa casera

7-3/4 oz. can Mexican hot-style
   tomato sauce
3-1/2 t. chicken bouillon
   granules

Remove seeds and membranes of both peppers for mild heat; remove half of the seeds for medium heat. Combine all ingredients in a 48-ounce blender; do not drain tomatoes. Process just until blended and smooth, but bits of green are still visible. Transfer to canning jars or plastic food containers; add lids. Keep refrigerated up to 3 weeks. Makes 3 to 4 cups.

Salsa is flavorful, naturally fat-free and tasty on so many
more foods than just tacos! Red or green, mild or hot, thin
or chunky style...try a spoonful of salsa as a topper for grilled
chicken, burgers and hot dogs, even egg dishes and casseroles.

Sunny-Day
Gatherings

Fresh Tomato Bruschetta

Jacki Smith
Fayetteville, NC

A great appetizer...the fresh tomatoes and basil taste like summer! My family loves this fresh bruschetta on garlic toasted baguettes and on grilled chicken breasts. It's a great way to use up extra tomatoes from the garden.

3 to 4 ripe tomatoes, diced
2 cloves garlic, pressed
3 T. fresh basil, minced
3 to 4 T. olive oil

sea salt and cracked pepper
    to taste
thinly sliced baguettes

In a bowl, combine tomatoes, garlic and basil; drizzle with olive oil. Season with salt and pepper. Set aside to marinate while toasting baguettes. To serve, spoon tomato mixture onto baguettes. Serves 6.

Retro Lemonade Ice Tea Punch

Teresa Verell
Roanoke, VA

This punch recipe has been a Verell family favorite for over 40 years! It is always served on family game and movie nights.

6 c. strong brewed iced tea,
    unsweetened
2 c. lemonade

1 c. ginger ale, chilled
crushed ice

In a one-gallon pitcher, combine iced tea, lemonade and ginger ale. Mix well; cover and refrigerate until thoroughly chilled. Serve over crushed ice. Makes 10 servings.

A merry heart doeth good like a medicine.
–Proverbs 17:22

Meatball Biscuit Roll-Ups

Anne Alesauskas
Minocqua, WI

One day, I had some leftover meatballs in my freezer and didn't know what to do with them, So I tossed this together and it made for an awesome recipe. Great for snacking, or for supper.

16.3-oz. tube refrigerated flaky
  layered biscuits
2 sticks string cheese
16 cooked meatballs, thawed
  if frozen

1 T. milk
1 T. grated Parmesan cheese
1/4 t. garlic powder
15-oz. jar pizza sauce, warmed

Separate each biscuit into 2 layers; set aside. Cut each string cheese into 8 pieces. Top each biscuit piece with a meatball and a piece of string cheese; wrap biscuit around them. Arrange biscuits seam-side down in a ungreased 8" round cake pan. Brush milk thinly over biscuits; sprinkle with Parmesan cheese and garlic powder. Bake at 375 degrees for 18 to 20 minutes, until golden. Serve with warmed pizza sauce for dipping. Serves 4 to 6.

Set up backyard games like croquet, cornhole and badminton for a party icebreaker that will bring all ages together.

Sunny-Day
Gatherings

Queso Dip

Karen Wilson
Defiance, OH

A delicious dip that can be made ahead for special occasions.
I like to transfer the dip to a slow cooker set on low to
keep it warm for serving.

3 T. butter
1 c. onion, finely chopped
2 10-oz. cans diced tomatoes
   with mild green chiles
14-1/2 oz. can stewed tomatoes

32-oz. pkg. pasteurized process
   cheese, cubed
16-oz. pkg. shredded Cheddar
   cheese
tortilla chips

Melt butter in a large saucepan over medium heat. Add onion; sauté until soft. Add tomatoes with juice; simmer until thickened, stirring occasionally. Reduce heat to low; add cheeses and stir until melted. Serve hot with tortilla chips. If making ahead, refrigerate; reheat and serve. Makes 8 to 10 servings.

Make your own crunchy pita chips for dipping. Cut
pita bread rounds into triangles, brush lightly with olive oil
and sprinkle with garlic salt or herbs. Bake at 350 degrees
for a few minutes, until crisp.

Spring & Summer
Recipes for Sharing

Sriracha Ranch Dressing & Dip

Harry Bastone
Littleton, CO

One day, I was looking for something different to break my routine and added the hot sauce to my salad dressing recipe. This makes a good dip for veggies and chicken nuggets, as well as a dressing for salad. It has become one of my favorites.

1 c. mayonnaise
1/2 c. sour cream
1/2 c. buttermilk
1/4 c. sriracha hot chili sauce
1 t. dried chives
1 t. dried parsley

1 t. dill weed weed
1/2 t. garlic powder
1/2 t. onion powder
1/4 t. salt
1/4 t. pepper

Whisk together all ingredients in a large bowl, adding more or less buttermilk to desired thickness. Cover and refrigerate for 30 minutes before serving. Makes about 2-1/4 cups.

Try something new with your next bowl of dip! Slices of zucchini, yellow summer squash and lightly steamed green beans, snow peas and asparagus spears are crunchy and full of flavor.

Sunny-Day *Gatherings*

Sweet Tea

Vicki Van Donselaar
Cedar, IA

This is such a refreshing drink when it's a hot and humid day here in southeast Iowa! Baking soda is the secret ingredient.

1/4 t. baking soda
12 regular tea bags
4 c. boiling water

1-1/2 c. sugar
12 c. cold water
ice cubes

Sprinkle baking soda into a one-gallon pitcher; add tea bags. Pour boiling water over tea bags. Cover and allow to steep for 15 minutes. Remove and discard tea bags; add sugar and stir until completely dissolved. Add cold water; stir again. Refrigerate until chilled; serve over ice cubes. Makes one gallon.

Crispy Roasted Chickpeas

Rita Morgan
Pueblo, CO

Perfect for nibbling while dinner is on the grill.

2 15-oz. cans chickpeas, drained
    and rinsed
2 T. olive oil

3/4 to 1 t. salt
2 to 4 t. favorite spice mix

Pat chickpeas very dry with paper towels; transfer to a ungreased baking sheet. Drizzle with oil; sprinkle with seasonings and toss well. Bake at 400 degrees for 25 to 30 minutes, until crisp, stirring occasionally. Transfer to a serving bowl. If desired, sprinkle and toss with more spices. Serve immediately. Makes 2 cups.

Cut cheese slices into simple stars, flowers or other fun shapes for a playful addition to a relish tray.

Spring & Summer
Recipes for Sharing

Southern-Style Deviled Eggs

Patricia Taylor
Louisville, KY

My sister and I enjoyed eating at a small cafe in town. Their deviled eggs were our favorite part of the menu, so we figured out how to make them. They were a hit with my friends at the school where I taught. My students even loved this "eggcellent" recipe. I like to arrange them on pretty vintage platters.

2 doz. eggs
1/8 t. salt
16-oz. pkg. sliced bacon
2 green onions, chopped

2 T. mayonnaise, or more
  as needed
coarse pepper to taste

Add eggs and salt to a large saucepan of boiling water; boil for 20 minutes. Drain; cover with ice water and let cool. Meanwhile, cook bacon in a skillet over medium heat until crisp. Drain bacon on a paper towel-lined plate. When cooled, separate the solid pieces of bacon from the fatty pieces. Tear solid pieces into small pieces in a large bowl; add onions and set aside. Peel eggs and cut in half horizontally; set aside egg whites on a platter. Add egg yolks to bacon in bowl. Add mayonnaise; mix thoroughly with a fork or an electric mixer on low speed until mixed well. Season with pepper. Spoon yolk mixture into egg whites. Cover and chill until ready to serve. Makes 4 dozen.

Toting deviled eggs to a cookout? Nestle the eggs in a bed of curly parsley or shredded lettuce to keep them from sliding around...they'll arrive looking as scrumptious as they taste!

Sunny-Day *Gatherings*

Cucumber Appetizers

Raksaa Meulenberg
Schenevus, NY

My grandma made this fresh springtime appetizer
for my 16th birthday...it was delicious!

36 slices white bread
8-oz. pkg. cream cheese,
  softened
1/4 c. sour cream
1/8 t. Worcestershire sauce

1/4 t. garlic powder
1/4 t. onion salt
1-1/2 cucumbers, sliced
Garnish: fresh dill sprigs

Cut out circles of bread with a biscuit cutter; set aside. In a small bowl, mix together cream cheese, sour cream, Worcestershire sauce and seasonings. Spread mixture on bread circles; top each with a slice of cucumber and a sprig of dill. Arrange on a platter; cover and chill until serving time. Makes about 3 dozen.

I have such fond memories of when I was little, enjoying the long, hot and lazy days of summer once school was out. Any small waterhole, creek or pond was where I could be found. I would set out early in the morning with my jar, fishing net and a small tin bucket that kept my sandwich safe from the ants, at least for a little while. Pretty or unusual rocks were stowed away in the bucket with the sandwich, as well as a nice piece of birch bark that I might find along the way, or the best find of all...a bird feather! It was so much fun to tease the crawfish and watch as they'd try to pinch your fingers, or tickle the tadpoles and watch them wriggle away. Nothing was ever captured without being released safe and sound. Growing up with nature taught me to respect and appreciate the gifts that Nature has to offer, and allowed me to pass this on to my own children.

–Janis Parr, Ontario, Canada

Spring & Summer
Recipes for Sharing

Easy Corn Relish

Steven Wilson
Chesterfield, VA

This corn relish is one of my favorite side dishes! We first tasted corn relish in New Jersey, years ago. I recreated this wonderful dish and now have it on the table often. It's perfect for our summer cookouts and gatherings, alongside other cold dishes like potato salad and coleslaw. It's got the perfect combination of sweet and tangy and adds a pop of bright color to the table. It's a very versatile dish that is a welcome addition at any time.

2 15-1/4 oz. cans low-salt-
   added corn, drained
   and rinsed
1/2 c. red pepper, finely chopped
1/2 c. red onion, finely chopped

1/4 c. cider vinegar
3 T. olive oil
1/4 c. sugar
1 t. salt
1/2 t. pepper

In a large bowl, combine corn, red pepper and onion; set aside. In a separate bowl, whisk together remaining ingredients. Pour over corn mixture and stir to combine. Cover and refrigerate for at least 3 hours, stirring mixture every hour. Store in a tightly covered container for up to one week. Makes 15 servings.

Set out a Mason jar filled with colorful striped
party straws, just for fun!

Sunny-Day
Gatherings

Grilled Bacon-Jalapeño Wraps

Ann Farris
Biscoe, AR

We love these little goodies anytime, anywhere....yum yum!

8-oz. pkg. cream cheese,
    softened
6 jalapeño peppers, halved
    lengthwise and seeded

12 slices bacon

Spread cream cheese to fill jalapeño halves. Wrap each jalapeño half with a bacon slice; secure with wooden toothpicks. Place on grill over high heat. Grill until bacon is crisp, turning occasionally. Makes one dozen.

Bacon-Wrapped Pineapple Bites

Jessica Kraus
Delaware, OH

These are so easy to make! The mixture of salty and sweet makes these so irresistible...always a hit at every party.

1 c. brown sugar
1 lb. sliced bacon, cut in half

20-oz. can pineapple chunks,
    drained

Add brown sugar to a shallow bowl. Dredge each piece of bacon in brown sugar. Place a pineapple chunk on the end of each bacon slice; roll up. Secure with a wooden toothpick. Arrange on a greased rack set in a rimmed baking sheet; sprinkle with remaining brown sugar. Bake at 375 degrees for 25 minutes, or until bacon is crisp. Makes about 2-1/2 dozen.

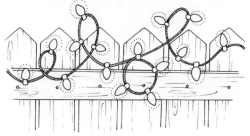

Wind sparkling white lights in your trees or around your patio for a twinkling firefly effect as the sun goes down.

Spring & Summer
Recipes for Sharing

Pineapple-Ham Cheese Ball

Shirley Howie
Foxboro, MA

The pineapple gives this cheese ball a slight sweetness, which nicely complements the savory ham. It comes together in a jiffy and is always a welcome addition to my holiday buffet!

2 8-oz. pkgs. cream cheese,
  softened
1/2 c. shredded sharp Cheddar
  cheese
8-oz. can crushed pineapple,
  well drained

1/2 t. seasoned salt
2/3 c. cooked ham, finely
  chopped
2 green onions, minced
1 c. pecans, finely chopped
assorted snack crackers

In a large bowl, stir together cheeses, pineapple and salt until well blended. Add ham and onions; stir to combine. Shape mixture into a ball. Wrap with plastic wrap; refrigerate for at least one hour. Just before serving, roll cheese ball in pecans. Serve with an assortment of crackers. Makes 12 servings.

Share the cheer! Invite party guests to bring along a can of tuna, a jar of peanut butter or another food item. Gather everything in a big wicker basket and drop off at a local food pantry.

Sunny-Day
Gatherings

Melon Salsa

Doreen Knapp
Stanfordville, NY

My niece came up to New York from Florida to visit, and she loved this salsa. It's so fresh and tastes delicious. You can also spoon it onto grilled pork chops, fish or even eggs for breakfast.

1 small ripe cantaloupe, peeled
   and finely diced
15-1/2 oz. can black beans,
   drained and rinsed
1 small jalapeño pepper, diced,
   seeds and ribs removed

1/2 c. red pepper, diced
1/2 c. yellow onion, diced
1 bunch fresh cilantro, chopped
juice of 2 limes
1/4 t. ground cumin
snack chips

Combine all ingredients except chips in a large bowl. Stir very well. Cover and refrigerate for 2 hours. Serve with chips. Serves 6 to 8.

Don't be shy...enter your best-ever recipe for pickles
or salsa in the county fair!

Spring & Summer
Recipes for Sharing

Jalapeño Cornbread Bites

Amanda Rentiers
Proctor, OK

We usually enjoy these with chili, but my kids could certainly eat a plate of just these! We love this recipe with Cheddar cheese, but any cheese you love would work well. If you like more heat, keep the seeds or add more jalapeños. If you like less heat, you can discard the seeds when chopping the jalapeños.

1 c. cornmeal	1 egg, beaten
1 c. all-purpose flour	1/4 c. oil
1/4 c. sugar	2 to 3 jalapeño peppers, diced
4 t. baking powder	1 to 2 c. shredded Cheddar
1 t. salt	cheese
1 c. milk	

In a large bowl, combine cornmeal, flour, sugar, baking powder and salt; mix well. Stir in milk, egg and oil until well combined. Gently fold in jalapeño peppers and desired amount of cheese. Scoop batter into 12 well-oiled regular muffin cups, or 24 mini muffin cups. Bake at 350 degrees for 15 to 20 minutes, until a toothpick comes out clean. Makes one to 2 dozen.

Set up a corn on the cob bar at your next cookout. Alongside a stack of grilled ears of sweet corn, set out bowls of herb butter, chopped chives, diced chiles and soft Mexican cheese... don't forget the salt and pepper!

Sunny-Day
Gatherings

Firecrackers

Diana Krol
Hutchinson, KS

My family loves these crackers! I like to serve them to accompany a cheese and sausage tray. My children and grandchildren will eat them by the handful. They are addictive! They have a little lingering heat... bet you can't just eat one!

16-oz. pkg. saltine crackers
1 c. oil
2 T. red pepper flakes

1/2 t. garlic powder
1-oz. pkg. ranch salad
   dressing mix

Add crackers to a large container with lid; set aside. In a small bowl, stir together remaining ingredients; pour over crackers. Cover tightly and let stand for one to 2 hours, gently turning container over every 15 minutes. Makes 10 to 12 servings.

Sparkling Lemonade

Sandy Ward
Anderson, IN

Garnish with lemon wedges, strawberries or blueberries.

12-oz. can frozen lemonade
   concentrate, thawed
2 c. pineapple juice, chilled

2 23-oz. bottles sparkling
   water, chilled
ice cubes

In a large pitcher, combine lemonade concentrate and pineapple juice; mix well. Cover and chill. At serving time, add sparkling water; serve over ice cubes. Makes 2 quarts.

A warm, melty cheese appetizer is irresistible! Slice Camembert or another soft cheese. Brush with olive oil and place directly on the grill until warmed through, about 2 minutes per side. Serve with crisp baguette slices.

Spring & Summer
Recipes for Sharing

Avocado-Black Bean Dip

Sara Voges
Washington, IN

This is my favorite summertime recipe! It's so fresh and easy...
delicious with tortilla chips, or spooned onto tacos.

2 15-1/2 oz. cans black beans,
   drained and rinsed
2 avocados, peeled, pitted
   and diced
1/2 jalapeño pepper, chopped

1/2 red onion, diced
1 bunch fresh cilantro, chopped
juice of 1/2 lime
1 T. ground cumin
salt to taste

Mix all ingredients in a large bowl. Cover and chill until serving time.
Makes 10 servings.

When making any dish with hot peppers as an ingredient,
it's always a good idea to wear a pair of plastic gloves to protect
your skin while cutting, slicing or chopping the peppers.
Just toss away the gloves when you're done.

Sunny-Day
Gatherings

Delectable Multi-Purpose Sauce

Pat Beach
Fisherville, KY

This is such an elegant sauce that can be used in so many ways. It is excellent as an appetizer, spooned over a block of cream cheese and served with crackers of your choice. It is also wonderful served on grilled steak, prime rib, roast beef and other cuts of beef.

17-oz. bottle chutney
14-oz. bottle catsup
12-oz. bottle chili sauce

11-oz. bottle thick steak sauce
10-oz. bottle Worcestershire
  sauce

Combine all ingredients in a large bowl; mix well. Cover and chill before serving. Keep refrigerated. Makes 2 quarts.

Fun polka-dotty paper napkins and matching plates make for
a table set with whimsy...and make clean-up a breeze!

Spring & Summer
Recipes for Sharing

Freezer Pickles

Debby Marcum
New Castle, IN

I have been making these pickles for over 25 years. We would take them on the sailboat to snack on during those warm summer days. They are best when eaten partially frozen.

7 c. cucumbers, thinly sliced	1-1/2 c. white vinegar
2 onions, thinly sliced	3 c. sugar
2 T. salt	1-1/2 T. celery seed

Combine cucumbers and onions in a large non-metallic bowl. Sprinkle with salt; cover and refrigerate for 2 hours. Transfer cucumber mixture to a colander and drain, but do not rinse. Return cucumbers to rinsed large bowl. In a separate bowl, whisk together vinegar, sugar and celery seed until sugar dissolves. Pour over cucumbers; mix well. Divide among plastic freezer bags; place bags on baking sheets. Place baking sheets in the freezer until cucumbers are frozen; keep frozen until ready to serve. Makes about 3 pints.

Easiest-ever sandwiches for party on a hot day...a big platter of cold cuts and cheese, a basket of fresh breads and a choice of condiments so guests can make their own sammies. Don't forget the pickles!

Sunny-Day
Gatherings

Art Crawl Olive Dip

Lindy Acree
Fairbanks, LA

I had this dip with crackers when I went to an "Art Crawl," and it is the best dip ever. It came to me by way of Paris...Texas, that is, not France! It is great served with any kind of cracker, but I like it the best with big corn chips.

8-oz. pkg. cream cheese,
  softened
1/2 c. mayonnaise
1 c. pecans, finely chopped

8-oz. jar Spanish green olives
  with pimentos, chopped
corn chips or crackers

In a bowl, blend cream cheese and mayonnaise; fold in pecans and olives. If mixture is too thick, add one to 2 teaspoons olive juice, until spreadable. Transfer to a serving bowl; serve with corn chips or crackers. Makes 24 servings.

Mom's Best Cheese Ball

Carolyn Gulley
Cumberland Gap, TN

This is my mom's go-to recipe for baby showers, bridal showers and family get-togethers. It's always a hit!

2 8-oz. pkgs. cream cheese,
  room temperature
1/4 to 1/2 c. green olives,
  chopped

1 T. dried, minced onions
2 2-1/2 oz. pkgs. dried, chipped
  beef, finely chopped
snack crackers or pita chips

Mix cream cheese, olives and onions in a bowl; roll into a ball or log. Spread chopped beef on wax paper; roll cheese ball or log in beef until covered. Serve with crackers or pita chips. Serves 10 to 15.

Scooped-out red and yellow peppers make fun containers
for dips and sauces.

Spring & Summer
Recipes for Sharing

Zucchini Pico Salsa

Stephanie Kemp
Lakeville, OH

We love to make this salsa as soon as the tomatoes and zucchini are ripe. It is a staple for us...I use it in salads and with fish as well as Mexican food and tortilla chips. We love it, and so does everyone who tries it! For another great taste, roast and peel the poblano pepper.

2 to 3 ripe tomatoes
1 zucchini, finely chopped
1 poblano pepper, chopped and
    seeds discarded
1/2 c. onion, chopped
Optional: 1 jalapeño pepper,
    diced and seeds discarded

2 T. fresh cilantro, minced
2 cloves garlic, minced
1/2 t. salt
1/2 t. pepper
3 T. lime juice

In a large bowl, combine all ingredients except lime juice; toss to mix. Add lime juice; toss to coat. Cover and refrigerate at least one hour before serving. Makes 4-1/2 cups.

Grill sweet or hot peppers for extra flavor. Slice peppers lengthwise into quarters and remove the seeds. Place peppers directly on a hot grill and cook until charred. Use tongs to drop peppers into a plastic zipping bag. Allow to cool; the peels will pull right off! Use right away, or freeze and use later.

Sunny-Day
Gatherings

Mock Margarita Punch

*Vickie
Gooseberry Patch*

*Perfect for a summer cookout! Serve in sugar-rimmed glasses,
with a sprig of fresh mint.*

12-oz. frozen lemonade
  concentrate, thawed
12-oz. frozen limeade
  concentrate, thawed

1/4 c. powdered sugar
6 c. crushed ice
2 ltrs. lemon-lime soda, chilled
Garnish: 2 thinly sliced limes

In a large plastic freezer bag, combine frozen juice concentrates,
powdered sugar and crushed ice. Seal tightly; freeze for at least one hour
to several days. At serving time, transfer to a punch bowl; no need to
thaw. Slowly add soda and lime slices. Serves 10 to 14.

Great Grape Lemonade

*Kimberly Redeker
Savoy, IL*

*Nothing's better than cold lemonade on a hot summer day! These
flavors really elevate the taste, making this a super-special
summertime sip. Use white grape juice, if desired.*

1/2 c. water
1/2 c. sugar
4 to 6 sprigs fresh mint

3/4 c. lemon juice
64-oz. bottle grape juice
Optional: additional fresh mint

In a small saucepan over medium heat, bring water, sugar and mint to
a boil. Stir until sugar dissolves; let cool. In a pitcher, combine sugar
mixture and fruit juices; cover and chill at least 2 hours. Mint sprigs
may be left in mixture to continue to add flavor; remove before serving.
Garnish with additional fresh mint, if desired. Makes 8 to 10 servings.

Spring & Summer
Recipes for Sharing

Crab Devils

Melanie Springer
Canton, OH

I first tried these tasty toasts at a party a long time ago and have been making them ever since. They are easy and delicious.

7-1/2 oz. can crabmeat, drained
   and flaked
3/4 c. mayonnaise
3/4 c. grated Parmesan cheese,
   divided
1 t. Worcestershire sauce
1/2 t. onion powder
salt and pepper to taste
5-1/4 oz. pkg. Melba toast
   rounds
Garnish: chopped fresh parsley

In a large bowl, combine crabmeat, mayonnaise, 1/2 cup Parmesan cheese, Worcestershire sauce and seasonings. Mix well. Spread on Melba toast rounds and sprinkle with remaining Parmesan cheese. Arrange on a broiler pan. Broil just until golden, watching closely to avoid burning. Garnish with parsley; serve warm. Makes about 3 dozen.

Watermelon is always a hit at cookouts! Chill the whole melon in an ice water-filled cooler, then cut into wedges for easy snacking. Set out a salt shaker for those who like it simple...add zest with Mexican chili-lime salt!

Sunny-Day
Gatherings

Summer Fun Fruit Dip

Kristy Wells
Ocala, FL

Here in Florida, we have access to some of the best fresh fruit. We know it's summertime when this fruit dip starts showing up at our house for barbecues and family gatherings! I'm asked for the recipe every time I make it and it's been a family favorite for years. It's very versatile and can be served as an appetizer or dessert. We especially like it with pineapple, mango, strawberries and blueberries. I hope you enjoy this easy and delicious dip.

8-oz. pkg. cream cheese, room
  temperature
7-oz. jar marshmallow creme

1-1/2 c. whipping cream, or 8-oz.
  container frozen whipped
  topping, thawed

Place cream cheese in a large bowl. Beat with an electric mixer on medium speed until softened. Add marshmallow creme; beat on high speed until blended together. If using whipping cream, add to bowl and beat on low speed until mostly combined. Turn to high speed and beat for about 5 minutes. If using whipped topping, use a spatula or large spoon to fold into mixture. Cover and chill before serving; best if refrigerated overnight. Serves 8 to 12.

Dining outdoors? Nestle cool, creamy dips into a bowl of ice
to keep the dip chilled.

Spring & Summer
Recipes for Sharing

Grilled Anytime Wings

*Paula Marchesi
Auburn, PA*

These grilled chicken wings have been a staple on our household for the past ten years. We like to grill all year 'round, even when there's snow on the ground. We make them for Memorial Day, 4th of July, Labor Day, Christmas & New Year's...birthday parties, too!

3 to 4 lbs. chicken wings,
  separated
1/2 c. olive oil
chili powder to taste

salt and pepper to taste
1/2 c. teriyaki sauce,
  or as needed

Place chicken wings in a large bowl; drizzle with oil. Sprinkle generously with seasonings; toss wings to coat well. Let stand while heating grill to medium. Arrange wings on grill; brush very lightly with teriyaki sauce. Cook, turning occasionally, for about 20 minutes, until wings are done, continuing to brush lightly with teriyaki sauce. Once cooked, wings may be heaped up on the cooler side of the grill until ready to serve. Serves 10.

Grilled Shrimp

*Crystal Shook
Catawba, NC*

Serve shrimp as an appetizer with your favorite cocktail sauce, or atop your favorite pasta.

1/4 c. olive oil
2 t. garlic, minced
1-1/2 t. fresh dill weed, minced
1/4 t. fresh thyme, minced

1/2 t. pepper
1 lb. large shrimp, peeled
  and cleaned

In a large bowl, whisk together oil, garlic, herbs and pepper. Add shrimp; turn to coat. Cover and refrigerate for one to 2 hours. Drain, discarding marinade. Arrange shrimp on a grill over medium-high heat. Cook for 3 to 5 minutes, turning occasionally, until done. Serves 4.

Sunny-Day
Gatherings

Strawberry Fruit Dip

Sherry Page
Akron, OH

Scrumptious! Serve with assorted fruit and small cookies.

1 c. strawberries, hulled
   and sliced
1/4 c. sour cream

1 T. sugar
1/4 t. vanilla
1/2 c. whipping cream

In a blender, combine strawberries, sour cream, sugar and vanilla. Process until smooth; set aside. In a small bowl, beat cream with an electric mixer on high speed until stiff peaks form. Fold into strawberry mixture. Cover and refrigerate for one hour. Makes about 1-1/2 cups.

Heavenly Fruit Dip

Jill Ball
Highland, UT

A better name for this would be "disappearing" fruit dip. It is gone in a flash! It's one of those dips that you'll want to lick the bowl clean. Try it and see!

8-oz. pkg. cream cheese,
   softened
14-oz. can sweetened
   condensed milk

1 t. lemon juice
cubed fresh fruit such
   as pineapple, apples,
   strawberries, grapes

In a bowl, beat cream cheese, condensed milk and lemon juice with an electric mixer on medium speed until well blended. Cover and chill for 3 hours before serving. Serve with fruit. Makes 20 servings.

Cucumber water is an oh-so easy, refreshing beverage. Simply add a cup of cucumber slices to a big pitcher, fill with water and chill for one to 2 hours before serving.

Spring & Summer
Recipes for Sharing

Garden Patch Squares

Myrna Barager
Ontario, Canada

This recipe was found in a pickle company's recipe booklet and it is so good! Can be varied according to the vegetables and pickle relish you like...it's just so versatile. I have used radishes, carrots and green, yellow and orange peppers as well as the veggies listed.

8-oz. tube refrigerated crescent roll dough
2 8-oz. pkgs. cream cheese, softened
1-oz. pkg. ranch salad dressing mix
1/2 c. pickle relish

1/4 c. mayonnaise
3/4 c. broccoli, chopped
3/4 c. red pepper, chopped
1/2 c. cauliflower, finely chopped
1/4 c. celery, chopped
1/4 c. black olives, chopped

Unroll crescent roll dough; press into the bottom of an ungreased 15"x10" jelly-roll pan. Press seams to seal. Pierce well with a fork. Bake at 350 degrees for 10 minutes, or until golden. Set aside to cool completely. Meanwhile, in a bowl, blend cream cheese, dressing mix, relish and mayonnaise until smooth. Spread evenly over baked crust. Combine remaining ingredients in another bowl; mix well. Scatter over cheese mixture, pressing in lightly. Cover with plastic wrap and chill before serving. Cut into small squares. Makes 3 dozen squares.

That beautiful season, the summer! Filled was the air
with a dreamy and magical light; and the landscape lay
as if newly created in all the freshness of childhood.

–Henry Wadsworth Longfellow

Sunny-Day *Gatherings*

Garlic Eggplant Dip

Lisa Ashton
Aston, PA

My mom used to make this often for parties, especially to use up the eggplant from my dad's garden. She passed this recipe down to us, and we always love to make it for family gatherings.

1 large eggplant
4 cloves garlic, minced
2 T. olive oil

6-oz. can tomato paste
1 egg, beaten
pita bread, cut into triangles

Line a baking pan with aluminum foil; place whole eggplant on pan. Bake at 350 degrees for about 30 minutes, until eggplant is deflated. Cool slightly; cut in half. Scoop out eggplant pulp into a bowl, discarding skin. Chop pulp into small pieces; set aside. In a skillet over medium heat, cook garlic in oil just until translucent. Stir in tomato paste; cook for 10 to 15 minutes, until hot and bubbly. Reduce heat to medium-low; stir in egg. Cook and stir until egg is set. Add eggplant pulp; cook until heated through. Serve warm with pita bread. Makes 8 servings.

Fill up a relish tray with crunchy fresh cut-up veggies as a simple side dish for sandwiches. A creamy salad dressing can even do double duty as a veggie dip and a sandwich spread.

Spring & Summer
Recipes for Sharing

Black-Eyed Pea Dip

Amy Moats
Hart, MI

This is a family favorite dip that we all call "Trash" but you'll call delicious. It's a must at all of our summer barbecues and holiday gatherings. It's especially popular while watching football games on television, and was my most-requested share for work potlucks and get-togethers. This dip is also delicious on salads. A hand-held chopper is very handy for dicing the peppers and onion.

16-oz. can black-eyed peas,
    drained and rinsed
15-1/2 oz. can black beans,
    drained and rinsed
15-oz. can white or yellow corn,
    drained and rinsed
1 green pepper, diced

1 yellow pepper, diced
1 red pepper, diced
1 orange pepper, diced
1 purple onion, diced
1 c. cider vinegar
1 c. sugar
scoop-type corn chips

In a large bowl, combine all canned and fresh vegetables; mix well and set aside. In a saucepan over medium heat, stir together vinegar and sugar; bring to a boil. Let boil for one minute, stirring constantly. Pour vinegar mixture over vegetable mixture. Cover and chill at least one hour before serving, or for best flavor, chill overnight. Serve with scoop-type corn chips. Serves 10 to 12.

For a quick & easy snack that everybody loves, nothing beats a big bowl of popcorn. Jazz it up with a sprinkle of grated Parmesan cheese or taco seasoning mix, or serve it the classic way, with butter and salt.

Desserts
for
Celebrating

Spring & Summer
Recipes for Sharing

One-Step Pound Cake

Kathy Oberst
Okeene, OK

I serve this cake every year at Easter. The lemon glaze is delicious! Slices are also scrumptious topped with strawberries and whipped cream.

2-1/4 c. all-purpose flour
2 c. sugar
1/2 t. salt
1/2 t. baking soda

1 t. vanilla extract
1 c. butter, softened
8-oz. container sour cream
3 eggs, beaten

Combine all ingredients in a large bowl. Beat with an electric mixer on low speed until mixed, then on medium speed for 2 minutes. Pour batter into a greased and floured 10" Bundt® pan. Bake at 325 degrees for 60 to 70 minutes, until cake springs back on top when touched. Set pan on a wire rack and cool for 12 to 15 minutes. Turn cake out of pan onto a plate; cool completely. Drizzle cooled cake with Lemon Glaze. Slice and serve. Makes 15 servings.

Lemon Glaze:

1 c. powdered sugar

1 to 2 t. lemon juice

Stir together powdered sugar and lemon juice to a glaze consistency.

For best results when baking, allow butter and eggs to come to room temperature. Just set them out on the counter about an hour ahead of time and they'll be ready.

Desserts
for Celebrating

Favorite Fruit Pizza

Tina Matie
Alma, GA

This is my mom's favorite dessert, so I make it for her every year for Mothers' Day. With a soft sugar cookie crust and fresh fruit, it's the best dessert...super-simple to make and is always a hit, especially with my mom. Share with your mom on Mothers' Day!

16-1/2 oz. pkg. refrigerated
    sugar cookie dough
8-oz. pkg. cream cheese,
    softened
1/2 c. sugar
1 t. vanilla extract
8-oz. container frozen whipped
    topping, thawed

assorted canned fruit like
    pineapple tidbits, mandarin
    oranges, maraschino cherries;
    fresh fruit like strawberies,
    grapes and blueberries

Spread cookie dough out evenly on a well-greased 14" round pizza pan. Bake at 350 degrees for about 13 to 15 minutes, until crust is just barely turning lightly golden. Let cool completely. In a large bowl, beat together cream cheese, sugar and vanilla; fold in whipped topping. Spread frosting evenly over cooled crust with a spatula. Arrange fruit over frosting; cover and chill until serving time. Cut into wedges to serve. Makes 12 servings.

Whip up some cool soda shoppe treats...enjoy a Pink or Brown Cow! Add a big scoop of vanilla ice cream to a tall glass, then top off with red pop or root beer.

Spring & Summer
Recipes for Sharing

Friendship S'mores

Amy Thomason Hunt
Traphill, NC

Wonderful to make with family and share with friends.

10 graham cracker sheets
1/4 c. marshmallow creme
1/4 c. chocolate hazelnut spread
6 1-oz. sqs. white melting
   chocolate
6 1-oz. sqs. semi-sweet
   melting chocolate

Garnish: candy sprinkles,
   chopped nuts, shaved
   chocolate, crushed graham
   crackers

Break graham cracker sheets in half. Spread 10 halves with marshmallow creme; spread remaining halves with hazelnut spread. Put together to form 10 sandwiches; set aside. In a microwave-safe bowls, melt white chocolate according to package directions. Dip 5 graham cracker sandwiches into melted white chocolate, coating completely. Arrange on a wax paper-lined baking sheet; sprinkle with desired toppings. Repeat with remaining sandwiches and semi-sweet chocolate. Makes 10 servings.

We find...delight in the beauty and happiness of children
that makes the heart too big for the body.
–Ralph Waldo Emerson

Desserts
for Celebrating

Light No-Bake Cherry Cheesecake

Leona Vinca
Eminence, KY

This is a great low-fat dessert. When I was first married, my mother-in-law made this with fresh strawberries. It was very good, but I liked the light canned cherries better. I like to use a chocolate crust, especially at the holidays...easy and delicious!

8 oz. pkg. fat-free cream cheese
1 c. calorie-free powdered
   sweetener
8-oz. container frozen light
   whipped topping, thawed

9-inch chocolate sandwich
   cookie crust
20-oz. can no-sugar-added
   cherry pie filling

In a large bowl, mix cream cheese and sweetener until well blended; fold in whipped topping. Spoon into crust, smoothing to the sides to make a little well in the center. Spoon pie filling into the well; cover and refrigerate. Cut into wedges. Makes 6 servings.

Apricot Shortbread Dessert

Lori Simmons
Princeville, IL

Use any pie filling you like, such as peach, raspberry or lemon. Apricot is my favorite.

3/4 c. butter, softened
1-1/3 c. sugar
2 eggs

2 c. all-purpose flour
20-oz. can apricot pie filling
cinnamon to taste

In a bowl, beat together butter and sugar. Add eggs, one at a time, beating until light and fluffy. Stir in flour. Press half of mixture into a buttered 13"x9" baking pan; spoon pie filling over dough. Drop remaining dough by spoonfuls over pie filling. Sprinkle with cinnamon. Bake at 325 degrees for 45 minutes, or until bubbly and golden. Makes 12 servings.

Spring & Summer
Recipes for Sharing

Grandma Peach's Peach Cobbler
Kimtoiya Sam
Indianapolis, IN

Summer was a special time for me. It always meant fresh peaches from my Grandma Peach's peach tree. We called her Grandma Peach because she made the best peach cobblers. Grandma would serve them with a scoop of ice cream...this dessert meant pure love. This cobbler can be made with ripe pears, nectarines, blueberries and blackberries too.

8 to 12 ripe peaches, peeled,
  pitted and thinly sliced, or
  2 15-oz. cans sliced cling
  peaches, drained
1 c. sugar
1/4 c. butter
1 t. vanilla extract
1/2 t. nutmeg
1/2 t. cinnamon
Optional: 1 T. all-purpose flour
  or cornstarch

Make Easy-Peasy Pie Crust; chill. Meanwhile, in a saucepan, combine peaches, sugar, butter, vanilla and spices. Simmer over medium heat for 15 to 20 minutes, until mixture thickens. If fruit mixture is too thin, stir in flour or cornstarch and cook until thickened. Divide dough into 2 balls; roll out dough 1/4-inch thick on a floured surface. Place one dough sheet into a 10" pie plate or round casserole dish; add peach filling and set aside. With a pizza cutter, cut remaining dough sheet into long strips. Cut several strips into pieces and add to peach filling. Layer dough strips on top in a lattice pattern; pinch to seal edges. Bake at 350 degrees for 40 to 55 minutes. Makes 8 to 12 servings.

Easy-Peasy Pie Crust:

1-1/4 c. all-purpose flour
1/4 t. salt
5 T. chilled butter, cubed
2 T. chilled shortening
4 T. ice-cold water

In a food processor, combine flour and salt. Pulse in cold butter, one to 2 cubes at a time; add cold shortening one teaspoon at a time until mixture binds and looks crumbly. Add water slowly; you may need a little more or less as dough forms. Form dough into a ball; cover and refrigerate for 45 minutes to one hour.

Desserts
for Celebrating

Amish Custard Pie

Jackie Smulski
Lyons, IL

Mid-June is the time of year that I have wonderful memories of past years and trips to Shipshewana, Indiana. It is a midwest gem of Amish country. This is a version of the treasured and classic custard pie. It's a breeze to put together in no time. Add some whipped cream for homespun goodness and toasted coconut for a nice little topping.

4 eggs	1/4 t. salt
1/2 c. sugar	1/8 t. nutmeg
2-1/2 c. whole milk	9-inch pie crust, unbaked
1/2 t. vanilla extract	

Lightly beat eggs in a large bowl. Add sugar, milk, vanilla, salt and nutmeg; mix well. Pour into unbaked pie crust. Bake at 400 degrees for 25 to 30 minutes, until lightly golden and set in the center. Cool completely; cut into wedges. Makes 6 to 8 servings.

Grandma's well-loved cookie cutters hold too many happy memories to be hidden in a drawer. Tie them to a grapevine wreath and add a big gingham bow for a delightful kitchen decoration.

Spring & Summer
Recipes for Sharing

Red, White & Blueberry Delight

Eleanor Dionne
Beverly, MA

This is a favorite for our July 4th barbecues. We begin with a parade in the morning, then go to the park, where there are games and goodies awaiting us. Later in the afternoon, we head back home for our traditional barbecue. This dessert is a perfect ending to the day.

14-oz. can sweetened
   condensed milk
1/3 c. lemon juice
2 t. lemon zest
16-oz. container plain yogurt
2 c. mini marshmallows

1/2 c. chopped pecans
1 pt. strawberries, hulled, sliced
   and well drained
1 c. blueberries, thawed and well
   drained if frozen

In a large bowl, combine condensed milk, lemon juice and zest; stir well. Stir in yogurt; fold in marshmallows and pecans. Spread half of mixture in an ungreased 13"x9" baking pan; arrange half of strawberries and blueberries on top. Cover with remaining condensed milk mixture; top with remaining berries. Cover with aluminum foil; freeze until firm. Remove from freezer 10 minutes before serving; cut into squares. Serves 15.

Invite friends to an ice cream social! Set out big tubs of ice cream in yummy flavors, plus all the toppings we love...hot fudge, nuts, chopped candy bars, sprinkles and whipped cream. Don't forget the maraschino cherries!

Desserts
for Celebrating

Homemade Vanilla Ice Cream

Lynnette Jones
East Flat Rock, NC

This is a family recipe that we have enjoyed using for many, many years. You can add chopped or cubed soft fruit, if you like. I usually subtract one cup of the whole milk for each cup of fruit added.

4 pasteurized eggs
1-1/2 c. sugar
6 c. whole milk
14-oz. can sweetened
   condensed milk

2 c. half-and-half
1 c. whipping cream
1 T. vanilla extract
1/2 t. salt

Whisk eggs in a large bowl; add sugar and stir well. Add remaining ingredients; mix well. Pour mixture into a 4-quart ice cream churn; process according to manufacturer's directions. Makes 15 to 20 servings.

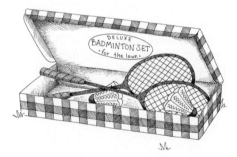

Summertime when I was ten years old meant my friend and me climbing the big tree in her front yard, sitting on the branches, singing as loud as we could. From "The Ants Go Marching" to "Sad Movies Make Me Cry", the songs and fun were endless. Afterwards, a competitive game of badminton would be played. It also meant playing dress-up with my friend, kissing our "boyfriends" (who happened to be a couple of old tennis rackets) and riding bicycles until dinnertime. Chasing fireflies, eating homemade ice cream, having wienie roasts, and camping at Fall River were certain this time of year. Oh, how the carefree days of a Kansas summer brings back wonderful memories, when everything was innocent and fun!

–Paula Anderson, Kingwood, TX

Spring & Summer
Recipes for Sharing

Mile-High Berry Pie

Clarice Hamer
Sun City West, AZ

One night I had a couple of friends over for dessert and served this light dessert. There were four of us...we ate the whole thing and it was wonderful!

1/2 c. butter, melted
1 c. all-purpose flour
1/4 c. brown sugar, packed
1/2 c. nuts, finely chopped
2 pasteurized egg whites

1 c. sugar
1 T. lemon juice
10-oz. pkg. frozen raspberries
   thawed and partially drained
1 c. whipping cream

In a bowl, combine butter, flour, brown sugar and nuts. Mix well; spread evenly in an ungreased 13"x9" baking pan. Bake at 350 degrees for 15 minutes; cool. In a large bowl, combine egg whites, sugar and lemon juice. Beat with an electric mixer on high speed until light and fluffy. Add berries and continue beating on high speed for 8 to 10 minutes; set aside. In another bowl, beat cream on high speed until soft peaks form. Fold whipped cream into berry mixture. Spoon into baked crust; cover and freeze for several hours. Let stand at room temperature for 10 minutes; cut into squares. Makes 10 to 12 servings.

Dress up a dessert with edible flowers...roses, daisies, violets and pansies are all pretty choices. Make sure your flowers are pesticide-free and rinse them well before using.

Desserts
for Celebrating

Jamen's Cherry Cobbler

Crystal Shook
Catawba, NC

*Every summer, my husband and I pick cherries off our tree.
This is the first thing we make with them...it's delicious
topped with vanilla ice cream!*

2 c. tart/sour cherries, pitted
2 c. sugar, divided
1 c. self-rising flour

1 c. whole milk
1 T. almond extract
1/2 c. butter, sliced

Spread cherries in a lightly greased 13"x9" baking pan; add one cup
sugar and toss to mix. Cover and refrigerate overnight, or until juicy.
In another bowl, mix together remaining sugar, flour, milk and extract.
Pour batter over cherries; do not stir. Dot with butter. Bake at
350 degrees for 50 to 60 minutes. Makes 10 servings.

Blueberry-Rhubarb Pie

Doug Shockley
Lincoln, NE

*I tried something a little different from a strawberry-rhubarb pie,
and so many people told me it was amazing. You can add
more sugar, but I like mine tart.*

2 9-inch pie crusts, unbaked
6 to 8 c. rhubarb, trimmed
   and chopped
1/2 c. blueberries

1/2 c. sugar
Garnish: vanilla ice cream or
   whipped topping

Arrange one pie crust in a 9" pie plate; set aside. In a bowl, mix together
rhubarb, blueberries and sugar; transfer to pie crust. Top with remaining
crust; pinch edges to seal and cut several slits with a knife tip. Bake at
400 degrees for 20 minutes. Reduce oven temperature to 350 degrees;
continue baking for 30 to 40 minutes. Cool; cut into wedges and
garnish as desired. Makes 8 servings.

Refrigerator Banana Split Dessert
Lynda Hart
Bluffdale, UT

When my daughter was young, I took her to her friend's birthday party. This is the dessert the little girl had requested instead of a cake. The kids loved it...you will too!

3/4 c. quick-cooking oats, uncooked
3/4 c. brown sugar, packed
1/2 c. all-purpose flour
1/2 c. butter, melted
16-oz. container frozen whipped topping, thawed and divided
3 ripe bananas, sliced

2 c. canned crushed pineapple, drained
1 c. strawberries, hulled and sliced
2 c. mini marshmallows
1/4 c. chocolate or caramel ice cream syrup
1/3 c. chopped nuts

In a bowl, combine oats, brown sugar, flour and melted butter. Mix well; press into a greased 13"x9" baking pan. Bake at 375 degrees for 15 minutes; cool completely. Spread 1/4 of whipped topping over cooled crust; layer sliced bananas over topping. Add another thin layer of whipped topping; layer with pineapple and strawberries. Spread another thin layer of whipped topping over fruit; cover with marshmallows. Spread remaining whipped topping over marshmallows; drizzle with ice cream syrup. Cover and chill for 3 hours. Just before serving, sprinkle with nuts. Cut into squares and serve. Serves 12.

To scoop ice cream in a jiffy, simply run the scoop
under very hot water first.

Desserts
for Celebrating

Rocky Road Squares

Glenna Kennedy
Ontario, Canada

This is my mom's special recipe that she made for my kids and hubby. They loved it! I have continued to make it every time the kids come home, or for special occasions for the hubby. Delicious!

1 c. semi-sweet chocolate chips
1 c. butterscotch chips
1 egg, beaten
1/2 c. butter

1 c. powdered sugar
10-1/2 oz. pkg. white or pastel
   mini marshmallows
Optional: flaked coconut

In a large saucepan, combine chocolate and butterscotch chips, egg, butter and powdered sugar. Cook and stir over low heat until chips are completely melted. Remove from heat; cool slightly. Add marshmallows; stir to coat well. Spread evenly in a 9"x9" baking pan coated with non-stick vegetable spray. If desired, sprinkle lightly with coconut. Refrigerate until serving time; cut into squares. Keep refrigerated. Makes one dozen.

Crunchy Butterscotch Fudge Bars

Gladys Kielar
Whitehouse, OH

These bars make wonderful gifts, or just enjoy them yourself!

6-oz. pkg. butterscotch chips
1/2 c. creamy peanut butter
4 c. crispy rice cereal
6-oz. pkg. semi-sweet
   chocolate chips

1/2 c. sugar
2 T. butter
1 T. water

Melt butterscotch chips with peanut butter in a heavy saucepan over low heat; stir until blended. Add cereal; mix well. Press half of mixture into a buttered 8"x8" baking pan; chill. Set aside remaining butterscotch mixture. Combine remaining ingredients in a heavy saucepan over low heat; stir until chocolate melts. Spread over chilled cereal mixture; top with remaining butterscotch mixture. Chill again; cut into bars. Makes 8 bars.

Spring & Summer
Recipes for Sharing

Sour Cherry Pie

Karen Wilson
Defiance, OH

The taste of summer in a pie crust! A little pie-baking tip...
the flour and sugar sprinkled into the unbaked crust prevent
the bottom crust from becoming soggy.

2 9-inch pie crusts, unbaked
1 t. all-purpose flour
1-1/2 c. plus 4 t. sugar, divided
1/3 c. cornstarch
1/4 t. salt

14-1/2 oz. can tart/sour cherries,
   drained and 1 c. juice reserved
1 T. butter
Optional: 1/4 t. almond extract,
1 T. milk

Arrange one crust in a 9" pie plate. Combine flour and one teaspoon sugar; sprinkle into bottom of crust and set aside. In a saucepan, combine 3/4 cup sugar, cornstarch and salt; stir in reserved cherry juice. Cook over medium heat for 4 to 5 minutes, until thickened. Remove from heat; stir in cherries, another 3/4 cup sugar, butter and extract, if using. Spoon filling into pie crust. Moisten the edges of bottom crust; top with remaining pie crust. Pinch to seal; flute edge of crust. Pierce crust several times with a knife tip. Brush crust with milk; sprinkle with remaining sugar. Bake at 350 degrees for 50 to 60 minutes, until bubbly and golden. Cool; cut into wedges. Makes 6 to 8 servings.

Fresh-picked cherries are one of summer's joys. No cherry pitter?
Remove the stems from the cherries, then push the end of a metal
drinking straw through the stem-end until the pit pops out.
The pointed end of a chopstick works too.

Desserts
for Celebrating

Strawberry-Rhubarb Upside-Down Cake

Lori Haines
Johnson City, TN

This recipe is so versatile! You can change the fruit and gelatin flavors to just about any kind of fruit you like. You don't have to flip this over to serve, but it is very beautiful on the top when you do. Serve warm, topped with ice cream.

1 qt. fresh strawberries, hulled
 and quartered
3 to 4 stalks rhubarb, trimmed
 and cut into 1-inch pieces
3-oz. pkg. strawberry gelatin mix
3 c. mini marshmallows
15-1/2 oz. pkg. yellow butter
 cake mix
4 eggs, beaten
1 c. milk
1/2 c. oil

In a one-gallon plastic zipping bag, combine strawberries and rhubarb. Sprinkle with dry gelatin mix; shake until well coated. Add fruit to a greased 13"x9" baking pan; spread out evenly in pan. Spread marshmallows over fruit; set aside. Prepare cake mix with eggs, milk and oil as package directs. Pour batter over marshmallows. Bake at 350 degrees for 25 to 30 minutes, until a toothpick tests done. Remove from oven; allow to cool slightly. Place another 13"x9" pan or a large platter over cake; carefully flip over. Spoon any ingredients remaining in pan onto cake. Cut into squares. Serve warm; store in refrigerator. Makes 12 servings.

Fresh rhubarb tends to absorb water easily, so clean stalks with a dampened paper towel rather than rinsing under running water.

Spring & Summer
Recipes for Sharing

Frosted Zucchini Brownies

*Amy Theisen
Sauk Rapids, MN*

A yummy treat to use up some garden zucchini. I like to serve these brownies topped with a scoop of vanilla ice cream...fantastic!

2 c. zucchini, grated
2 c. sugar
1 t. salt
1 t. vanilla extract
2 eggs, beaten

1/2 c. oil
1-1/2 t. baking soda
1/4 c. baking cocoa
2 c. all-purpose flour
Optional: 1/2 c. chopped walnuts

In a large bowl, mix all ingredients except optional walnuts in order listed. Pour batter into a greased 13"x9" baking pan. Bake at 350 degrees for 20 to 30 minutes; let cool. Spread with Cocoa Frosting. Sprinkle with walnuts, if using; cut into bars. Makes one dozen.

Cocoa Frosting:

1/2 c. margarine, sliced
1/4 c. baking cocoa
5 T. milk

3 c. powdered sugar
1 t. vanilla extract

In a heavy saucepan over medium heat, combine margarine, cocoa and milk. Bring to a boil, stirring often; remove from heat. Stir in powdered sugar and vanilla until smooth; cool.

Bake up some brownies or bar cookies, then cut, wrap and freeze individually. Later you can pull out just what you need for a last-minute treat.

Desserts
for Celebrating

Brownies' Coconut-Filled Macaroons

Marcia Shaffer
Conneaut Lake, PA

Our little Brownie troop from years ago loved to play in the backyard, under the trees and in them. When they finally came in, their little faces and hands dirty with play, the girls thought nothing could be better than my chocolate macaroons and a glass of cold milk!

4 egg whites
1/4 c. water
2/3 c. sugar
2 t. vanilla extract
1 T. all-purpose flour

1/2 t. salt
2 1-oz. sqs. unsweetened
   baking chocolate, melted
2-1/2 c. flaked coconut

Combine egg whites and water in a large bowl. Beat with an electric mixer on high speed until stiff, but not dry. Beat in sugar and vanilla; set aside. Combine flour and salt in a cup; add to egg white mixture, folding in carefully. Fold in melted chocolate and coconut. Drop batter by teaspoonfuls onto parchment paper-lined baking sheets. Bake at 325 degrees for 25 to 30 minutes, until lightly golden. Cool completely. Makes 2 to 2-1/2 dozen.

Découpage Mom's favorite cookie or candy recipe onto the lid of a cookie tin, then line with a lacy napkin. A thoughtful container for delivering goodies to a lucky friend or relative.

Spring & Summer
Recipes for Sharing

Blackberry Dumplings

Beckie Apple
Grannis, AR

My Granny Wilkins was half Creek Indian and a fantastic little woman who raised eleven children! She and Grandpa raised 90 percent of everything their large family ate. They had a fruit orchard which included Arkansas blackberries. Her blackberry dumplings were rich, sweet and delicious.

8 c. water
1/4 t. salt
3 qts. blackberries

1/4 c. butter
3-1/2 c. sugar

Make dough for Dumplings; set aside. In a 5-quart stockpot, combine water and salt. Bring to a boil over high heat; add blackberries. Reduce heat to medium; simmer for 25 minutes. Set a colander over a large saucepan. Strain berries and seeds out of juice; use only the juice, discarding berry mixture. Add butter and sugar to juice; simmer over medium heat for 5 minutes. Bring to a slow rolling boil. Add dumplings, a few at a time, stirring after each batch, until all dumplings are added. Reduce heat to simmering; cook and stir for 5 minutes. Serve warm. Serves 4 to 6.

Dumplings:

4 c. all-purpose flour, divided
1/2 t. baking powder
1/2 t. salt

1/2 c. oil
1/4 c. cold water

Combine 3-1/2 cups flour, baking powder and salt; mix well. Add oil and cold water; stir to make a soft dough. Add more cold water by tablespoonfuls, if needed. Sprinkle remaining flour on countertop; roll out dough to 1/8-inch thickness. Cut dumplings into strips, 2 inches long by one inch wide.

Desserts
for Celebrating

Beach Apple Bread

Lindy Acree
Fairbanks, LA

*We call this Beach Apple Bread because the first time we made,
it we were on a family beach vacation. We were tired of the same
old breakfast foods. My niece had this recipe and we made it...it was
wonderful! Now we make it and it brings back such lovely memories
of that summer at the beach with my family. Everyone knows when
you say Beach Apple Bread, it is the bread that is melt-in-your-mouth
good! Enjoy the best apple bread ever.*

2 c. sugar
2 eggs, beaten
1-1/2 c. canola oil
2 t. vanilla extract
3 c. all-purpose flour
1 t. baking soda

1 t. salt
1 t. cinnamon
3 c. Granny Smith or Gala apples,
    peeled, cored and chopped
1 c. chopped pecans

In a large bowl, blend together sugar, eggs, oil and vanilla; set aside.
In another bowl, mix together flour, baking soda, salt and cinnamon.
Add to sugar mixture; stir well. Fold in apples and nuts. Divide batter
between 2 greased and floured 9"x5" loaf pans. Bake at 350 degrees for
one hour. Let cool; turn loaves out of pans and slice. Makes 2 loaves.

Best Friends Day is June 8...a great day to share homebaked
goods and a cup of tea with your dearest friend!

Spring & Summer
Recipes for Sharing

Campfire Cherry Cobbler

Marian Forck
Chamois, MO

We enjoy making this dessert when camping...it is so good. We let it cool a little and add some vanilla ice cream. Delicious!

21-oz. can cherry pie filling
15-1/2 oz. pkg. white or yellow
   dry cake mix

1 c. plus 2 T. lemon-lime soda
1/4 to 1/2 c. butter, sliced
cinnamon to taste

Spray the bottom of a 12" Dutch oven with non-stick vegetable spray. Line bottom of pan with aluminum foil; spray again. Spoon pie filling into pan; cover with dry cake mix. Drizzle with soda. Dot with butter; sprinkle with cinnamon. Arrange 8 to 10 hot charcoal briquettes or coals in campfire; set covered pan on top. Arrange another 8 to 10 briquettes on lid. Cook for 35 to 40 minutes, until golden, checking after 30 minutes. Serves 6 to 8.

Grilled Chocolate Dessert Wraps

Gladys Kielar
Whitehouse, OH

You will love these...they take just a few minutes on the grill.

4 8-inch flour tortillas
1/2 c. creamy peanut butter
1 c. mini marshmallows

1/2 c. mini semi-sweet
   chocolate chips
Garnish: vanilla ice cream

Spread each tortilla with 2 tablespoons of peanut butter. Sprinkle half of each tortilla with 1/4 cup marshmallows and 2 tablespoons chocolate chips. Roll up, enclosing toppings. Wrap each tortilla in heavy-duty aluminum foil, sealing tightly. Grill, covered, over low heat for 5 to 10 minutes, until heated through. Carefully unwrap tortillas; place on dessert plates and serve with ice cream. Serves 4.

Desserts
for Celebrating

Pound Cake Pie Packets

Lisa Ellsworth
Sparta, MO

We enjoy this around the campfire as a tasty alternative to s'mores. We love it with peach, blueberry, strawberry and cherry pie filling. Our oldest son Gabriel has requested it as his pie for Thanksgiving and gave it its name!

1 loaf pound cake
softened butter to taste
21-oz. can favorite fruit
   pie filling

Garnish: powdered sugar

Cut pound cake into 8 equal slices. Lightly spread butter on one side of each slice. Place each slice butter-side down on a piece of aluminum foil; spoon pie filling to cover the slice. Top with second piece of cake, butter-side up. Wrap foil around each "sandwich" and place it on grill or grate, indirectly over medium heat campfire coals. Cook until warmed through, about 5 to 10 minutes. Remove from foil; sprinkle with powdered sugar. Serves 4.

Grilled Banana Split

Sandy Coffey
Cincinnati, OH

S'mores are always yummy when you're grilling, but we like these grilled banana splits. Super-simple and super-delish...a heavenly dessert right before your eyes!

4 ripe bananas
1/4 c. mini marshmallows
1/4 c. semi-sweet chocolate chips

Garnish: whipped cream,
   maraschino cherries

Peel back one section of each banana skin lengthwise; scoop out 1/4 of banana and reserve for another use. Stuff with marshmallows and chocolate chips. Press banana peels back into place; wrap tightly with aluminum foil. Grill for about 3 to 5 minutes, turning over several times. Carefully remove foil; top with whipped cream and cherries. Serves 4.

Spring & Summer
Recipes for Sharing

Strawberry Bars

Cindy Mitchell
Maroa, IL

My husband and daughters all love these bar cookies! A family favorite for many years...we like strawberry the best, but other flavors of preserves may be used. Wonderful with homemade preserves, and good with store-bought preserves too.

2 c. all-purpose flour
1 c. sugar
1 t. lemon zest
1/2 c. softened butter

1/2 c. butter-flavored shortening
1 egg, lightly beaten
1 c. chopped walnuts
3/4 c. strawberry preserves

In a large bowl, combine flour, sugar and lemon zest. Cut in butter and shortening with a pastry cutter or a fork until well blended. Stir in egg and nuts. Pat half of dough into a greased 13"x9" baking pan; set aside remaining dough. Spread preserves to within 1/2 inch of edges. Crumble remaining dough evenly over top. Bake at 350 degrees for 45 minutes, or until lightly golden. Set pan on a wire rack to cool; cut into squares. Cover to store. Makes 2 dozen.

Planning dessert for a graduation party or wedding shower?
Bite-size treats are such fun for sampling...they'll go farther, too!
Cut brownies and bar cookies into one-inch squares and place
each in a paper candy cup. Arrange them in a basket or on a platter.

Desserts
for Celebrating

6-Minute Chocolate Chip Cookies

Tyce Smith
Henderson, KY

Spend less time in the kitchen and more time in the sunshine! These amazing cookies are done in no time and are sure to please. Feel free to use any type of chocolate chips you like, and some chopped walnuts, too.

1/2 c. butter, melted	5 T. sugar
1 egg, beaten	3 T. cornstarch
1/2 t. vanilla extract	1/2 t. baking soda
1-1/4 c. all-purpose flour	1/2 t. salt
7 T. brown sugar, packed	1 c. semi-sweet chocolate chips

In a large bowl, stir together butter, egg and vanilla; set aside. In a separate bowl, stir together remaining ingredients except chocolate chips; mix well. Add flour mixture to butter mixture; stir well. Fold in chocolate chips. Drop dough by rounded tablespoonfuls onto ungreased baking sheets. Bake at 475 degrees for 6 to 7 minutes. Cool on wire racks. Makes 1-1/2 dozen.

Hosting a summer tea party for your best friends? Bring Grandma's Sunday going-to-church hats out of their boxes and arrange several on hat stands for a whimsical display.

Judy's Lemonade Cake

Judy Borecky
Escondido, CA

This recipe came from our squadron commander's wife in 1961, when we were in the U.S. Air Force. I have been making it ever since! For special occasions, top each piece of cake with a dollop of whipped cream and a lemon drop candy.

15-1/4 oz. pkg. lemon cake mix	1 c. water
3.4-oz. pkg. instant lemon	1/2 c. oil
pudding mix	1 t. lemon extract
4 eggs, beaten	Optional: 1-1/2 t. poppy seed

In a large bowl, combine cake and pudding mixes, eggs, water, oil, extract and poppy seed, if desired. Beat with an electric mixer on high speed for 2 minutes. Pour batter into a 12"x12" baking pan sprayed with non-stick vegetable spray. Bake at 350 degrees for 26 minutes, or until a toothpick inserted in the center tests clean. Remove from oven; poke holes in cake with the handle of a wooden spoon. Drizzle with Lemon Glaze. Cut into squares. Makes 20 servings.

Lemon Glaze:

1 c. powdered sugar	2 T. butter, melted
1/3 c. frozen lemonade	1 t. lemon zest
concentrate, thawed	

Stir together all ingredients to a glaze consistency.

To make sure that a frosted cake stays its prettiest, refrigerate it for one hour before slicing...it'll give the frosting time to firm up.

Desserts
for Celebrating

Malt Shoppe Dessert

Vicki Van Donselaar
Cedar, IA

This unique frozen dessert is often brought to our spring and summer family reunions. There are never any leftovers!

1 c. graham cracker crumbs
3 T. butter, melted
2 T. sugar
1/2 gal. vanilla ice cream,
   softened
1-1/2 c. malted milk balls,
   crushed and divided

4 T. milk, divided
1 c. whipping cream
6 T. marshmallow creme
6 T. instant chocolate malt
   powder

Combine graham cracker crumbs, butter and sugar in a bowl; mix well. Pat into a 13"x9" glass baking pan and set aside. In a separate bowl, blend together ice cream, one cup crushed malted milk balls and 2 tablespoons milk; spread over graham cracker crust. Cover and freeze until frozen. Shortly before serving time, beat cream with an electric mixer on high speed until soft peaks form; set aside. In another bowl, blend marshmallow creme, remaining milk and malt powder; fold into whipped cream and spread over ice cream. Top with remaining malted milk balls; cut into squares and serve. Makes 15 servings.

Dress up desserts of all kinds with a toss of candy sprinkles. They're available in a rainbow of colors and shapes...look for them in the baking aisle at the supermarket or craft store.

Spring & Summer
Recipes for Sharing

Karen's Iced Orange Cookies

Emilie Britton
New Bremen, OH

*A recipe from a special friend...these cookies are full
of wonderful orange flavor!*

1 c. milk
1 T. vinegar
1 t. baking soda
1 c. shortening

2 c. sugar
3 eggs, beaten
5-1/4 c. all-purpose flour
zest and juice of 1 navel orange

In a large bowl, combine milk, vinegar and baking soda; let stand for 5 minutes. Add remaining ingredients and mix well. Drop dough by tablespoonfuls onto lightly greased baking sheets. Bake at 350 degrees for 10 minutes. Cool cookies on a wire rack; spread with Orange Icing. Store in an airtight container. Makes 2 dozen.

Orange Icing:

16-oz. pkg. powdered sugar
1 T. butter, melted

zest and juice of 1 navel orange

Mix all ingredients until smooth.

Super-simple ice cream sandwiches! Place a scoop of softened ice cream on the flat bottom of one cookie. Top with another cookie; press gently. Serve immediately, or wrap and freeze for up to one week.

Desserts
for Celebrating

Fresh Plum Bread

Judy Phelan
Macomb, IL

We love summer-ripe plums! The best plums to use are the purple prune plums at our local farmers' market. They come from southern Illinois and are the sweetest tasting plums!

1 c. ripe plums, halved, pitted and chopped	1/2 t. vanilla extract
1-1/2 c. plus 1 T. all-purpose flour, divided	2 eggs, beaten
	1/4 t. baking soda
1/2 c. margarine	1/2 t. salt
1 c. sugar	1/3 c. plain yogurt
	1/4 c. brown sugar, packed

In a bowl, sprinkle plums with one tablespoon flour; toss to coat and set aside. In a separate large bowl, beat margarine, sugar and vanilla until light and fluffy. Beat in eggs. In another bowl, combine remaining flour, baking soda and salt; mix well. Stir flour mixture into egg mixture, alternating with yogurt; stir until smooth. Lightly fold in plums. Pour batter into a 9"x5" loaf pan coated with non-stick vegetable spray. Sprinkle brown sugar over batter. Bake at 350 degrees for 45 to 50 minutes, until a toothpick inserted into center comes out clean. Set pan on a wire loaf and let cool for 10 to 15 minutes. Turn loaf out of pan and slice. Makes one loaf.

To give warm-from-the-oven bread a sweet, shiny glaze, brush with honey. It also absorbs moisture and keeps the bread fresh longer.

Spring & Summer
Recipes for Sharing

Mama Sue's Sour Cream Cookies *Jodie Stadelman*
Amherst, NY

My mom made these the first time my fiancé came over. Mom taught us how to make them and they've been a hit ever since. Sweet and delightful...scrumptious!

1 c. butter, softened
1-1/2 c. sugar
2 eggs, beaten
1 T. vanilla extract

1 c. sour cream
3-1/2 c. all-purpose flour
1-1/2 T. baking powder
1/8 t. salt

In a large bowl, blend butter and sugar; add eggs and vanilla. Fold in sour cream. Add flour, baking powder and salt; mix well. Scoop dough by tablespoonfuls onto parchment paper-lined baking sheets. Bake at 350 degrees for 12 to 15 minutes. Let cool for 30 minutes; spread with Glaze. Makes 2 dozen.

Glaze:

3 c. powdered sugar
3 T. butter, melted

1 T. vanilla extract
2 to 3 t. milk

Stir together all ingredients to a glaze consistency.

Bring lots of plastic flying disks to your next picnic. They make great paper plate holders at lunch and are fun for the kids afterwards!

Desserts
for Celebrating

Peanut Butter Fudge
Ice Cream Pie

Karen Wilson
Defiance, OH

Ice cream pies are the perfect summer dessert. They are so simple to make and can be made ahead...just pull them out of the freezer at party time!

1/2 c. creamy peanut butter
1/4 c. honey
1-1/2 qts. vanilla ice cream, softened
9-inch graham cracker crust
3/4 c. hot fudge sauce, warmed and divided

3/4 c. chopped cashews, divided
Garnish: whipped topping, additional hot fudge sauce and cashews

In a large bowl, stir together peanut butter and honey; fold in ice cream. Spread half of mixture in graham cracker crust. Drizzle with half of hot fudge sauce; sprinkle with half of cashews. Repeat layering. Cover and freeze for 8 hours, or overnight. Garnish with whipped topping, additional hot fudge sauce and cashews. Cut into wedges. Makes 6 to 8 servings.

Looking for an alternative to peanut butter in recipes? Try sun butter, made from sunflower seeds, or soy nut butter, made from soybeans. If your child has a peanut allergy, check with the doctor first, to be on the safe side.

Spring & Summer
Recipes for Sharing

Julie's Chocolate Brownies

Julie Gallagher
Attleboro, MA

*I have been making this recipe since I was about
12 years old. They're still wonderful!*

2 c. all-purpose flour	4 eggs, beaten
2 c. sugar	1 c. butter, melted
6 T. baking cocoa	1 t. vanilla extract
1 t. baking powder	1 c. chopped nuts

In a bowl, mix together flour, sugar, baking cocoa and baking power.
Add eggs, melted butter and vanilla; stir well. Fold in nuts. Pour batter
into a greased 13"x9" baking pan. Bake at 350 degrees for 20 to
25 minutes, until a toothpick tests done. Cool; cut into squares.
Makes 16 brownies.

Lazy-Day Cookie Bars

Sandy Coffey
Cincinnati, OH

*For a quick dessert or just for fun with the kids,
this recipe is super-fun and easy.*

15-1/4 oz. pkg. yellow cake mix	5 T. butter, melted
2 eggs, beaten	2 c. semi-sweet chocolate chips

In a large bowl, combine dry cake mix, eggs and butter; mix well. Fold
in chocolate chips. Pour batter into a greased 13"x9" baking pan. Bake
at 350 degrees for 20 minutes. Cool and cut into bars. Makes 2 to
3 dozen.

The sun does not shine for a few trees and flowers,
but for the wide world's joy.
–Henry Ward Beecher

Desserts
for Celebrating

Indoor S'mores

Vicki Van Donselaar
Cedar, IA

*Camping season may be over, or maybe it's just a rainy day,
but you can still make these yummy s'mores.*

8 c. bite-size sweetened graham
    cereal squares
6 c. mini marshmallows, divided
1-1/2 c. milk chocolate chips

6 T. butter
1/2 c. light corn syrup
1 t. vanilla extract

Place cereal in a large heat-proof bowl; set aside. In a large saucepan over low heat, melt 5 cups marshmallows, chocolate chips, butter and corn syrup; stir until smooth. Remove from heat; stir in vanilla. Pour over cereal in bowl; mix quickly and stir in remaining marshmallows. Transfer to a lightly greased 13"x9" baking pan. Let stand until set; cut into bars. Makes 1-1/2 dozen.

Walnut Squares

Melanie Springer
Canton, OH

Easy, quick and so good!

1 egg, beaten
1 c. brown sugar, packed
1 t. vanilla extract
1/2 c. all-purpose flour

1/4 t. baking soda
1/4 t. salt
1 c. chopped walnuts

Stir together egg, brown sugar and vanilla in a bowl. Sir in flour, baking soda and salt; mix in walnuts. Spread dough in a greased 8"x8" baking pan. Bake at 350 degrees for 18 to 20 minutes; will be soft in the center. Cool; cut into squares. Makes 16 squares.

Packing for a camping trip? Be sure to bring a big bag of marshmallows for toasting...kids of all ages will come running!

Spring & Summer
Recipes for Sharing

Punchbowl Cake

Judy Scherer
Benton, MO

*I like to bake my own cake for this party-perfect dessert.
My mother and grandmother used to use a store-bought pound cake
or angel food cake. Either way, it's delicious!*

18-1/4 oz. pkg. yellow or
   white cake mix
2 5-oz. pkgs. instant vanilla
   pudding mix
5 c. milk
6 ripe bananas, sliced
2 20-oz. cans crushed
   pineapple, drained

2 21-oz. cans cherry pie filling
6-oz. pkg. flaked coconut
16-oz. container frozen whipped
   topping, thawed
Optional: 1/2 c. chopped walnuts

Prepare and bake cake mix according to package directions for 2 layers.
Let cool. Prepare pudding mixes with milk according to package. Tear
cake into bite-size pieces; add half of cake pieces to a large glass
punchbowl or trifle bowl. Layer with half of pudding, half of bananas,
one can pineapple, one can pie filling and half of coconut. Repeat
layering. Top with whipped topping and walnuts, if using. Cover and
chill until serving time. Serves 16 to 24.

Sugar-Free Ice Cream Sandwiches

Joyce Roebuck
Jacksonville, TX

*This tastes like real ice cream...you'll be surprised! With less sugar,
it's good for diabetics and also to have on hand for the grandkids.*

1.3-oz. pkg. instant sugar-free
   vanilla pudding mix
1-1/2 c. 1% or skim milk
12-oz. container frozen light
   whipped topping, thawed

14.4-oz. pkg. reduced-fat
   chocolate or plain graham
   crackers

Whisk together dry pudding mix, milk and whipped topping; mixture
will be thick. Spread 1/2-inch thick on one graham cracker; top with
another cracker. Wrap individually in plastic wrap and freeze. Makes
about 14 sandwiches.

Desserts
for Celebrating

Strawberry Trifle

Pieterina Oskam
British Columbia, Canada

This is a very cheerful and colorful dessert...
a perfect ending to a holiday meal!

3.4-oz. pkg. instant vanilla
    pudding mix
3 c. milk
1-1/2 c. whipping cream
1 angel food cake, torn into
    bite-size pieces

2 c. fresh strawberries, hulled
    and sliced
Optional: additional strawberries,
    melted chocolate

In a large bowl, whisk together pudding mix and milk for 2 minutes; cover and chill. In a large bowl, beat cream with an electric mixer on high speed until soft peaks form; set aside. In a large glass trifle bowl, layer half each of cake pieces, pudding, whipped cream and strawberries. Repeat layering. If desired, garnish with more strawberries or melted chocolate. Cover and refrigerate until serving time. Makes 8 servings.

Dress up scoop & serve desserts with a paper
cocktail parasol...how fun!

INDEX

INDEX

INDEX

Sandwiches

Sides

Soups-Chilled

Soups-Hot